Family Law: Tips & Traps
Hints, Help and Specimen Orders

Family Law: Tips & Traps
Hints, Help and Specimen Orders

District Judge Clive Million

ℐ Family Law

Published by Family Law
A publishing imprint of Jordan Publishing Limited
21 St Thomas Street
Bristol BS1 6JS

British Library Cataloguing-in-Publication Data

A catalogue record for this book is available from the British Library.

ISBN 978 1 84661 045 5

Typeset by Letterpart Ltd, Reigate, Surrey
Printed and bound in Great Britain by Antony Rowe, Chippenham, Wiltshire

Contents

The Purpose of these Notes

These notes provide guidance on common practice points that arise in district judges' work in the Principal Registry of the Family Division.

They are intended as a ready reference guide. The aim is to reduce common technical and practice errors.

They cover in particular special procedure petitions, private law money cases, directions and paperwork, court listing, non-molestation orders, disclosure of addresses and information, and some Children Act orders and directions.

Most of the problems and points identified will be familiar and relevant to other family law court centres.

Some specimen common form orders are included.

This guidance was first written to speak directly to Principal Registry district judges and deputy district judges. In this public edition, intended for a wider audience, the direct imperative 'voice' of the original is retained.

1 Introduction

1-01 Check List for Court Work and Paperwork

1-01.1 The following applies to all court work and paperwork:

- **Date and sign any order, comment or request you make.**

- **Use your full normal signature, not just initials.**

- **Identify an order clearly. Use: 'Order' or 'O/'.**

- **Distinguish an order from a comment, or a request. Orders have to be drawn by the clerk. A comment or request does not.**

- **Do not use 'approved', if you are making an order. How are the staff to know whether that is an order or not?**

- **Make clear the beginning and end of an order. Start with the date, then put the recitals and order, then sign immediately underneath it.**

- **Always check the court file, including previous orders, before making an order.**

- **Are solicitors acting, or is it a litigant in person?**

  - If there are solicitors acting, are they on the record?

  - If not, is there a 'notice of acting' filed with the application?

  - If the solicitor is not on the record and there is no notice of acting, the client has to sign personally, though the solicitors may countersign.

  - Note that a petitioner, though acting in person, may use a solicitor's address for service in the petition in some circumstances *(see para 6-01.3 below)*.

1-02 Paperwork 'Stops'

1-02.1 When you examine an application, you may find that it is not possible to deal with it without returning it to the applicant or his or her solicitors for them to rectify errors or to clarify certain matters, ie 'stop' the application.

1-02.2 In so far as it is possible to do so, you should note all the points at the same time, so as to avoid successive or multiple 'stops'. Endorse your brief comments on the back sheet side of the application/draft order. Date and sign the comments. If the error is a trivial one, for example a typographical mistake, correct it yourself rather than send it back.

1-03   Family Proceedings: The Principal Rules

1-03.1   The Family Proceedings Rules 1991, as amended, (FPR) are the principal rules.

1-03.2   The FPR also incorporate[1] the Rules of the Supreme Court 1965 (RSC) and the County Court Rules 1981 (CCR) as they were on 25 April 1999 (ie. the day before the Civil Procedure Rules 1998 (CPR) came into force on 26 April 1999).

1-03.3   The RSC and CCR are therefore frozen in time and included in the FPR to fill any procedural gaps there may be in the family rules. Note, in particular, that enforcement in family proceedings is still governed by the RSC and CCR, not the CPR. But some of the CPR rules about experts[2] apply to ancillary relief applications, and some of the CPR rules about costs assessment[3] now apply to family proceedings.

1-04   Adoption: The Current Rules

1-04.1   The other main rules in family proceedings are the Family Procedure (Adoption) Rules 2005, as amended on 1 October 2007 – FP(A)R 2005.

1-04.2   The FP(A)R 2005 apply to adoption proceedings issued from 30 December 2005, when the Adoption and Children Act 2002 came into force.

1-04.3   The FP(A)R 2005 are a self contained code, applicable to all new adoption proceedings in the High Court, county court and magistrates' court.

1-04.4   There are some later references to some aspects of adoption orders (in particular editing of reports and disclosure of addresses, *see para 16 below*), but it is not the intention of this guide to provide a detailed treatment of adoption proceedings.

1-05   Adoption: The Old Rules

1-05.1   You may need, rarely now, to consider the Adoption Rules 1984 (AR 1984). These apply to adoption proceedings issued before 30 December 2005. The AR 1984 incorporate the RSC and CCR, in a similar way to the FPR. The 1984 Rules are of diminishing relevance. They may however have to be considered if, for example, a (now adult) subject child applies for information relating to an adoption order made under the old rules.

---

[1]   FPR r 1.3.
[2]   FPR r 2.61C.
[3]   FPR r 10.27.

2 Matrimonial and Civil Partnership Proceedings: An Overview

2-01 Marriage and Civil Partnership: Substantive Law

2-01.1 The principal statute for matrimonial law is the Matrimonial Causes Act 1973. This was a largely consolidating statute following the major changes introduced by the Divorce Reform Act 1969.

2-01.2 The Civil Partnership Act 2004 (CPA 2004) came into force on 5 December 2005. For dissolution, separation and nullity in civil partnerships, the 2004 Act takes[1] as its model the basic substantive law used by the Matrimonial Causes Act 1973 (MCA 1973) in marriages.

2-01.3 The language used in the substantive law of civil partnership (including dissolution, separation and financial ancillary relief) derives closely from that of marriage. There are some obvious and necessary differences.

2-01.4 All foreign countries recognise marriage. Few recognise same sex civil partnerships.

2-02 Marriage/Civil Partnership: Procedural Law

2-02.1 The previously existing procedures for petitions, applications and orders under the Matrimonial Causes Act 1973 have also been adapted for use in proceedings under the Civil Partnership Act 2004.[2]

2-02.2 The petition procedure now applies both to matrimonial (heterosexual) proceedings and civil partnership (same sex) proceedings. Procedurally, they are identical. For most practical purposes the proceedings can be thought of as the same. But there are differences – see later.

2-02.3 A 'cause' under the amended Family Proceedings Rules 1991 includes a 'matrimonial cause' and a 'civil partnership cause'.

2-02.4 Both are begun by petition, and 'ancillary relief' includes financial claims under both the MCA 1973 and CPA 2004.[3]

2-02.5 *Table 1 (para 3-01 below)* summarises and compares the grounds and facts for dissolution, separation and nullity and the basic procedural terminology used.

---

[1] CPA 2004 Chapter 2, ss 37 et seq.
[2] FPR r 2.1 – as amended on 5 December 2005 by the Family Proceedings (Amendment) (No 5) Rules 2005 (SI 2005/2922).
[3] FPR r 2.51B (as renumbered from 5.12.2005).

3   Marriage and Civil Partnership: Dissolution, Separation and Nullity

3-01   ***Table 1: Comparison of Grounds, Facts and Terminology***

Matrimonial	Civil Partnership
Dissolution/Separation	
dissolution: irretrievable breakdown and a 'fact'	*dissolution:* irretrievable breakdown and a 'fact'
separation: a 'fact' only	*separation:* a 'fact' only
adultery	–
behaviour	behaviour
2 years desertion	2 years desertion
2 years separation and consent	2 years separation and consent
5 years separation	5 years separation
Nullity – Void	
within prohibited degrees – marriage	within prohibited degrees – civil partner
under 16 years	under 16 years
formation requirements disregarded	knowing lack of registration requirements
already married or a civil partner	already a civil partner or married
not respectively male and female	not both of the same sex
polygamous marriage and domicile	–
–	a child (16 or 17) and no parental etc consent
Nullity – Voidable	
non consummation (incapacity)	–
non consummation (wilful refusal)	–
invalid consent	invalid consent
mental disorder and unfit	mental disorder and unfit
communicable venereal disease	–
pregnant by another	pregnant by another
interim gender recognition certificate	interim gender recognition certificate
acquired gender	acquired gender
Procedural Names	
ancillary relief	ancillary relief
avoidance of dispositions	avoidance of transactions
decree of divorce	dissolution order
decree of judicial separation	separation order
decree of nullity	nullity order
decree nisi	conditional order
decree absolute	final order
maintenance pending suit	maintenance pending outcome
petition	petition
spouse	civil partner

4　　　**Petitions: Special Procedure – A Basic Guide**

4-01　　*Introduction*

4-01.1　　35 years ago and more the evidence in all petitions for matrimonial divorce or separation had to be heard in open court. A special (paperwork) procedure was then introduced for a restricted class of petitions (2 years separation and consent). In 1978 the 'special procedure' became 'general' when it was applied to all undefended petitions, but it retains the old name.

4-01.2　　All undefended petitions for matrimonial divorce or judicial separation or civil partnership dissolution or separation (and one type of nullity petition) may now be dealt with as paperwork.[1] This is the 'special procedure' (SP). All but a handful of petitions are now dealt with in this way.

4-01.3　　An undefended nullity petition based on the voidable ground that an interim gender recognition certificate has been issued to either party after the marriage or civil partnership may be dealt with under the special procedure.[2]

4-01.4　　All defended petitions and all but that one type of nullity petition, whether defended or undefended, must be heard in open court by a judge[3] (not a district judge).

4-02　　*Table 2: Petitions where the Special Procedure may be used*

Matrimonial – Undefended	**Civil Partnership – Undefended**
Divorce/Judicial Separation	**Dissolution/Separation**
adultery	–
behaviour	behaviour
2 years desertion	2 years desertion
2 years separation and consent	2 years separation and consent
5 years separation	5 years separation
Nullity – Voidable	**Nullity – Voidable**
interim gender recognition certificate	interim gender recognition certificate

4-03　　*Publicity and Inspection of Documents*

4-03.1　　Under the special procedure, the only court hearing which takes place for the matrimonial decree or civil partnership order itself (that is, excluding ancillary proceedings for such things as money claims) is the formal pronouncement of the

---

[1]　FPR r 2.24(3).
[2]　FPR r 2.24(3); s 12(g) MCA 1973; and s 50(1)(d) CPA 2004.
[3]　FPR r 2.32(1); 'judge' does not include 'district judge' FPR 1.2(1) Interpretation.

decree or order. This must be in open court.[4] Just as a marriage or civil partnership is formed in public, so its judicial ending is public.

4-03.2   Because the pronouncement must be in open court, the cause must first appear in the public court list. That list is made public (on the Court Service website) the day before.

4-03.3   This vestige of the open court hearing is seen in the rule[5] which permits 'within 14 days after the pronouncement of the decree or civil partnership order' any person to 'inspect the [SP] certificate and the evidence filed ... except the statement of arrangements and may bespeak copies on payment of the prescribed fee'.

4-03.4   The decree or order made in open court may also be inspected and copied, without leave of the court,[6] at any time.

4-03.5   Commonly, celebrity divorces and civil partnership dissolutions attract journalists to the SP pronouncement hearing when they then ask for copies of the permitted petition documents.

4-03.6   Any person is entitled, on payment of a fee, to take copies of:

(within 14 days of the pronouncement hearing)

- the district judge's special procedure certificate

- the affidavit in support of the petition (but not the statement of arrangements, even if exhibited to the affidavit)

- (BUT NOT IF it is nullity based on an interim gender recognition certificate)

(at any time)

- the matrimonial decree or civil partnership order pronounced in open court: that is –

(matrimonial)

- a divorce decree nisi

- a nullity decree nisi

- a judicial separation decree;

---

4   FPR r 2.36(2).
5   FPR r 2.36(4).
6   FPR r 10.20(3).

(civil partnership)

- a dissolution conditional order

- a nullity conditional order

- a separation order.

5   Petitions: Special Procedure Paperwork

5-01   'Directions for Trial'

5-01.1   In an undefended suit, the SP referral is sent to a district judge with an SP certificate which is blank except for a stamped signature on the 'directions for trial' part of the form. When this happens, 'directions for trial' have been given.

5-01.2   Before directions for trial, leave is not required to file an amended or supplemental petition (so long as the petition is undefended).[1]

5-01.3   Once directions for trial have been given (ie. the SP referral is made) leave is required before a petition (or Answer and Cross-Petition) may be amended, or a supplemental petition filed. (See also: the sections on *Supplemental and Amended Petitions - para 7 below*).

5-02   The Time before Issue of Petition

5-02.1   A separation petition may be issued within a year of marriage or partnership, but a divorce or dissolution petition can be issued only after a year. A clear year must elapse before the issue of a divorce or dissolution petition, ie excluding the day of marriage.[2] So a divorce or dissolution petition issued on the first anniversary of the marriage is a day too soon.

5-02.2   Beware: A separation petition presented within one year cannot therefore be amended to seek divorce or dissolution, and would have to be stopped.

5-03   Is There an Answer on File?

5-03.1   Always check the file to see if an Answer has been filed. Occasionally a petition which is in fact defended is referred by mistake to a district judge under the special procedure.

5-03.2   There may be clues which suggest that there may be an Answer. The acknowledgment of service (AOS) filed by the respondent (or co-respondent) may state an intention to defend the petition. A previous order on the file may refer to an Answer, or have given leave for one to be filed. Check whether an Answer has been filed, but overlooked.

5-03.3   Often a respondent will file an acknowledgment of service with a statement attached to it which disputes the factual allegations in the petition. Typically, this will be in respect of the behaviour allegations. Most such statements are sent 'for the record' and are not intended as a formal Answer, and this is usually made clear in the AOS. In any event, a formal Answer requires the payment of a filing fee, unless the respondent is fee exempt.

---

[1]   FPR rr 2.11(1) and 2.14.
[2]   See *Warr v Warr* [1975] Fam 25.

5-03.4   Check any statements lodged with the AOS because, even if not a formal Answer, occasionally they raise questions which go to the root of the court's jurisdiction to hear the divorce (see 'Jurisdiction' below), or because they raise doubts about the truth of the main fact of divorce (eg. in a 2 year or 5 year separation petition, that the parties have not been separated for the necessary time). It may then be necessary to ask the petitioner to explain in writing or on affidavit any apparent discrepancy.

5-04   An Answer which is Struck Out

5-04.1   Not infrequently, after an Answer is filed and the suit has become defended, the parties later agree to allow the suit to proceed undefended. This will require an order that 'the Answer is struck out'. The Answer itself will then still remain on the court file as a document, but it can be ignored.

5-04.2   See the later section *'Resolving Defended Petitions or Cross Petitions' – para 8 below*, which deals in more detail with defended suits which then proceed undefended.

6   The Contents of the Petition

6-01   Introduction

6-01.1   The contents of the petition must contain the information required by Appendix 2 of the FPR.[1] The next paragraphs follow the same order as the form of a petition.

6-01.2   The following paragraphs refer usually to marriages. This is for economy of expression. But the procedural requirements apply equally to civil partnership matters. Also the substantive law on the grounds and facts necessary to prove relationship breakdown in matrimonial causes applies equally to civil partnership, subject to some obvious and necessary differences.

6-01.3   Note that in a matrimonial or civil partnership cause, a petitioner, though acting in person, may give as his address for service the name and address of a solicitor provided that the solicitor (a) has given him legal advice and assistance, and (b) agrees.[2] The petitioner, however, will remain on the court record as acting in person. The court file may then be marked 'I/P' and the address 'c/o' the solicitor's address. The commonest example is where a party is receiving publicly funded 'Legal Help'.

6-02   Marriage or Civil Partnership: Title of the Parties

6-02.1   A recent President's Direction[3] provides that:

(1)   when a party to a matrimonial (and now civil partnership) cause has changed his or her name since marriage (or civil partnership), the name currently used by that party should appear first on any petition, answer and statement of arrangements followed by 'formerly known as ..... (married name)';

(2)   in any decree, order, or notice the parties should be described by their full current names only;

(3)   details of the parties in any court list should include only the initials and surname of their current name;

(4)   titles such as Mr, Mrs, Miss etc should be omitted.

6-02.2   This Direction was prompted by the Gender Recognition Act 2004 which came into force on 4 April 2005. The Direction is given further purpose by the implementation of the Civil Partnership Act 2004.

---

[1]   FPR r 2.3.
[2]   FPR App 2 para 4(c) – Contents of the Petition.
[3]   President's Direction of 5 April 2005: The Gender Recognition Act 2004. Procedure – Title of the Cause. [2005] 2 FLR 122.

6-03 *The Marriage or Civil Partnership Certificate*

6-03.1   A valid marriage or civil partnership certificate is required (FPR 2.6(2)) If leave was given to file the petition without such a certificate, it must be filed before the district judge's certificate is signed.

6-03.2   Marriages or civil partnerships formed in England and Wales are proved by the production of the original marriage or civil partnership certificate or a copy issued by the Registrar General's Office.[4] A photocopy or other copy certificate is not acceptable.

6-03.3   The evidence required to prove a marriage or 'an overseas relationship' (civil partnership) formed outside England and Wales is dealt with in FPR 10.14. A certificate in a foreign language must be 'accompanied by a translation, certified by a notary public, or authenticated by affidavit'.

6-03.4   Certificates of religious ceremonies are not usually accepted. Church certificates issued in Eire are not accepted; the Irish State issues formal marriage certificates.

6-03.5   If no marriage certificate exists, the marriage must nevertheless be proved. This problem will only arise with foreign marriages. Proof is usually by an affidavit of law. If the marriage was performed by local custom, the petitioner must also provide an affidavit giving the necessary facts (usually describing the marriage ceremony) which the affidavit of law proves as a valid marriage.

6-03.6   If the details of the place of marriage given in the petition differ from those in the certificate, it is not necessary to 'stop' the SP. The staff will take the details from the certificate, which will be assumed to be correct.[5]

6-03.7   It is not usually necessary to stop the SP if the names of the parties differ between the petition and the marriage certificate, unless it is the surname and no explanation is given in the petition. The new advisory form of the petition includes an initial paragraph in which it is expressly stated whether either the petitioner or respondent has changed their name since the marriage/civil partnership.

6-03.8   Some previous guidance suggested that, where names differed between the petition and marriage certificate, the SP certificate could be signed but with a note on the stop form to state 'certificate subject to the petitioner certifying correct names'. This is no longer a satisfactory technique. The court staff do not have reliable systems to monitor proper compliance with such a direction. The better practice is to require the petitioner to provide an explanation before the SP certificate is signed.

---

4   Marriage Act 1949 s 65(3); CPA 2004, s 156.

5   See the Secretary's Circular dated 23 June 1978: Family Division Directions p C12. The Family Division Directions are in a black plastic covered ring binder. Whilst sometimes still useful, these ring binders are no longer kept up to date when changes occur.

6-04   *Two Marriage Ceremonies*

6-04.1   Divorce dissolves the status of marriage, not the ceremony.[6]

6-04.2   Sometimes a couple go through 2 ceremonies of marriage – typically a ceremony abroad and then one in England and Wales. This is usually because couples coming to this country wish to show the UK authorities that they are, beyond doubt, validly married. This raises the question: which ceremony created the valid marriage?

6-04.3   On separation, many (including some lawyers and judges!) think that it is necessary to petition for nullity in respect of the 'invalid' ceremony. This is a mistake.

6-04.4   Where there are 2 ceremonies it is best to include details of both in the petition, with a statement of which is said to be the valid marriage. The court must decide which of the two ceremonies created the marriage, and only that ceremony should be recited in the decree.

6-05   *The Marriage or Partnership Address*

6-05.1   The last address at which the parties lived together as husband and wife (or civil partners) should be given.

6-06   *Jurisdiction of the Court – Introduction*

6-06.1   The petition must state the basis on which the court has jurisdiction, and the necessary facts. If this is omitted or is insufficient, stop the SP and ask for more information.

6-06.2   Under the European Council Regulation, Brussels II (revised), the court is under a duty to consider of its own motion whether it has jurisdiction to deal with the petition.[7] Check the file and especially the acknowledgment of service to see if any such questions may be identified. If so the petition may have to be stayed whilst further information is sought.

6-06.3   The Regulation controls the jurisdiction of the court where[8] a spouse:

(1)   is habitually resident in the territory of a Member State; or

(2)   is a national of a Member State or, in the case of the United Kingdom and Ireland, has his or her 'domicile' in the territory of one of the latter Member States.

---

[6]   *Thynne (Marchioness of Bath) v Thynne (Marquess of Bath)* [1955] P 272; [1955] 3 All ER 129.
[7]   Art 17 European Council Regulation (EC) No 2201/2003.
[8]   Art 6 European Council Regulation (EC) No 2201/2003.

6-06.4 The Council Regulation does not apply to Denmark, even though it is an EU Member State. Denmark has opted out of it.

6-06.5 The country of domicile or the dates and addresses of habitual residence must be stated in the petition in cases where the Council Regulation does not apply (FPR App 2 para 1(d)).

6-06.6 The following paragraphs summarise the required facts for jurisdiction in marriage *(see para 6-07 below)* and partnership petitions *(see para 6-08 below)*.

6-07   *Jurisdiction: Matrimonial Petitions – (Brussels II revised)*

6-07.1 The courts of England and Wales have jurisdiction[9] in divorce, nullity and judicial separation petitions ('matrimonial matters') filed on or after 1st March 2001 where any one of the following applies:[10]

(1) The petitioner and respondent are **both habitually resident** in England and Wales.

(2) The petitioner and respondent **were last habitually resident** in England and Wales **and one** of them still **resides** there.

(3) The **respondent** is **habitually resident** in England and Wales.

(4) The **petitioner** is **habitually resident** in England and Wales **and** has **resided** there for at least **a year immediately before** the filing of the petition.

(5) The **petitioner** is **habitually resident and domiciled** in England and Wales **and** has **resided** there for at least **6 months immediately before** the filing of the petition.

(6) The petitioner and respondent are **both domiciled** in England and Wales.

(7) If no court of a contracting state has jurisdiction under the Council Regulation and

    (a) either the petitioner or the Respondent is domiciled in England and Wales; or

    (b) (in the case of nullity only) either spouse died before the date proceedings begun and either was at death domiciled in England and Wales or had been habitually resident in England and Wales throughout the period of 1 year ending with the date of death.

---

[9] Section 5 Domicile and Matrimonial Proceedings Act 1973, as amended by the Council Regulation.

[10] Council Regulation (EC) No 2201/2003 – (in force on 1 March 2005) – concerning jurisdiction and the recognition and enforcement of judgments in matrimonial matters and the matters of parental responsibility, repealing Regulation (EC) No 1347/2000.

6-07.2   The court (including a district judge) may grant a stay of the proceedings if it appears that the court does not have jurisdiction under the Council Regulation to hear the petition.[11]

6-08   *Jurisdiction: Civil Partnership Petitions*

6-08.1   The courts of England and Wales have jurisdiction in civil partnership petitions for a dissolution, nullity or separation order filed on or after 5 December 2005 where any one of the following applies:[12]

(1)   The court has jurisdiction under 'section 219 regulations'[13] (in effect the same circumstances as for matrimonial petitions above – see Brussels II revised).

(2)   If no other court has, or is recognised as having, jurisdiction under section 219 regulations, and

(a)   either civil partner is domiciled in England and Wales on the date when proceedings are begun; or

(b)   the parties registered as civil partners in England and Wales and it appears to the court to be in the interests of justice to assume jurisdiction in the case; or

(c)   (in the case of nullity only) either civil partner died before the date proceedings begun and either was at death domiciled in England and Wales or had been habitually resident in England and Wales throughout the period of 1 year ending with the date of death.

6-08.2   The effect is, as far as possible, to make the jurisdiction in civil partnership proceedings co-extensive with that in matrimonial proceedings.

6-08.3   Note the additional 'interests of justice' ground. This may be applicable where, for example, parties who registered as civil partners in this jurisdiction are now living abroad in a country which does not recognise such relationships.

6-08.4   The court (including a district judge) may grant a stay of the proceedings in similar circumstances as a stay of a 'matrimonial matter' under the Council Regulation.[14]

---

[11]   FPR r 2.27A.

[12]   Section 221 CPA 2004.

[13]   The regulations made under s 219 CPA 2004 are the Civil Partnership (Jurisdiction and Recognition of Judgments) Regulations 2005 (SI 2005/3334) which make provisions corresponding to those in Brussels II revised – Council Regulation (EC) No 2201/2003.

[14]   FPR r 2.27AA. See also the Family Proceedings (Civil Partnership: Staying of Proceedings) Rules 2005 (SI 2005/2921).

6-09   Occupation and Residence

6-09.1   The occupation and residence of both the petitioner and the respondent must be given. The petitioner's address may be omitted with leave.

6-09.2   Unless leave has been given to omit the petitioner's address, it must be given and the SP should be stopped so that it can be obtained. It may be necessary for the petition to be re-served. Sometimes the address of the respondent is omitted because it is unknown but if this is the case, the petition will say so.

6-10   Omitting the Petitioner's Address

6-10.1   An application to omit the petitioner's address from the petition is made by affidavit, on lodging the petition. The usual reason is fear of harassment or violence from the respondent. When the order is made, the petitioner's affidavit (which will include the address) is then placed on the file in a sealed envelope, marked 'not to be opened without leave of the court'.

6-10.2   In these circumstances, obviously, an alternative address for service of documents on the petitioner must be provided – usually a solicitor, or (if the petitioner is in person) a family member or friend.

6-11   Children

6-11.1   The petition must state whether or not there are any 'children of the family'. These are defined as children of the parties or children treated as children of the family.[15] If there are, it must state the number of children and their full names and dates of birth (if they are under 18), or that he or she is over 18.

6-11.2   Petitions must state whether a child over 16 is receiving instruction at an educational establishment or undergoing training for a trade, profession or vocation.

6-11.3   If there are children of the family under 16, or a child of the family who is 16 or 17 and in education or undergoing training, then the petition must be accompanied by a 'statement of arrangements for children'.[16]

6-11.4   See also the section 'Statement of Arrangements for Children' *(para 6-25 below)*.

6-11.5   Details must also be given (if known) of any other children born to the wife or either civil partner during the marriage or civil partnership.

6-11.6   If a child of the family has been omitted from the petition, then the petition will have to be amended and re-served. If the child is included but the details omitted then written information from the petitioner (for example, in the affidavit in support) will usually be sufficient.

---

[15]   MCA 1973 s 41; CPA 2004 s 75(3).
[16]   FPR r 2.2(2) and Form M4.

6-12   *Other Proceedings (Past or Present)*

6-12.1   The petition must disclose whether there are or have been any other proceedings 'with reference to' the marriage or civil partnership or any of the children or <u>between the parties</u> about any property.

6-13   *Other Proceedings for Dissolution or Separation*

6-13.1   If the other proceedings affecting the validity of the marriage or partnership have been disposed of, then there should be some evidence of this. If the other proceedings were in the PRFD, the court file should be tied together with the SP file and reference can be made to it directly. If the proceedings are elsewhere, a copy of the order disposing of the proceedings should be sought from the petitioner, if not already provided.

6-13.2   If the other proceedings have not been disposed of, then (generally) they should be, either:

(1)   consolidated, if both are intended to continue; or

(2)   stayed or dismissed, before continuing the SP petition.

6-13.3   This can usually be done by a consent order. For consolidation, the order is made in both petitions to be consolidated *(see para 7-06.4 below)*. For stay or dismissal, the order is made in the petition which is to be stayed or dismissed *(see para 7-04.3 below)*. The SP should be stopped until this is done. This is simpler to deal with where both petitions were issued in the same court (PRFD). If one petition is in another court, then an order from that court dismissing the other petition may be obtained. Alternatively, one set of proceedings can be transferred to the PRFD (or the PRFD petition to the other court), and the orders in both petitions then coordinated in the same court.

6-13.4   It is important that all the proceedings affecting the validity of the marriage or partnership be coordinated. This avoids a 'petition race', where one party seeks to get 'their' final order first. A marriage or civil partnership can only be dissolved once, so there can only ever be one decree absolute (final order).

6-13.5   If the other proceedings were issued in another court by the respondent and are dormant, there may be circumstances when no further action need be taken, for example, when the respondent can no longer be traced. It may then cause needless expense and delay to require the petitioner to make applications to the other court for a stay or dismissal.

6-13.6   Where a petition has not been dismissed, another petition <u>by the same petitioner</u> shall not be presented without leave (FPR 2.6(4)). This rule does not prevent <u>the respondent</u> from presenting his or her own petition – but if this happens, consider consolidation *(see paras 6-13.2 above and 7-06.4 below)*.

6-13.7 The commonest example of the petitioner being allowed to present 2 concurrent petitions is where the first petition is defended or controversial, and the parties then agree to proceed on a different agreed or uncontested fact.

6-13.8 The court would then order that:

Order: Leave to Present a Second Petition

ORDER
1. Even though the present petition is not disposed of, the petitioner may present a second petition based on [adultery; 2 years separation etc].
2. On presentation of the second petition this petition No. FD08D05555 shall be stayed and dismissed on the pronouncement of the decree nisi in the second petition

6-13.9 On rare occasions it may emerge that a second petition has been filed without leave. The court may make an order allowing the second petition to proceed even though it was filed without leave. However an order should also then be made in the first petition that:

Order: Stay and Dismissal of an Existing Second Petition

ORDER
The (first) petition No FD07D05555 is stayed and dismissed on the pronouncement of the decree in the (second) petition No FD08D09999.

6-14   Dissolution: The Ground – Irretrievable Breakdown

6-14.1 Technically, the only 'ground' for divorce or dissolution of a marriage or civil partnership is that it 'has broken down irretrievably'.[17] This must be pleaded in petitions for divorce or dissolution. In addition a 'fact' must be proved (one of 5 in marriage, one of 4 in civil partnership – *see para 3-01 above, Table 1*). Conveniently, but confusingly, the 'facts' are often referred to as 'grounds'.

6-14.2 Note that the 'facts' in s 44(5) of the Civil Partnership Act 2004 are set out in a different order to s 1(2) of the Matrimonial Causes Act 1973.

6-14.3 The wording of both the 'ground' and 'fact' must be specifically and accurately pleaded. If not the petition must be amended and re-served.

6-15   Separation: No Ground – A 'Fact' Only

6-15.1 In separation petitions, irretrievable breakdown is not required, only a 'fact'.[18]

---

[17]   MCA 1973 s 1(1); CPA 2004 s 44(1).
[18]   MCA 1973 s 17(1); CPA 2004 s 56(1).

6-15.2   If a separation petition is amended to seek divorce check that 'irretrievable breakdown' is included in the amendment.

6-15.3   A separation petition presented within one year cannot be amended to seek divorce or dissolution, and would have to be stopped *(see para 5-02 above)*.

6-16   The 'Facts': Adultery

6-16.1   Adultery is a 'fact' available in marriage dissolution and separation, but not civil partnership.[19] Sex between a same sex couple outside the marriage is not adultery, but may prove 'behaviour'. Sex (heterosexual or same sex) outside the civil partnership is not adultery either, but may prove the 'fact' of behaviour.

6-16.2   The petition must state that the respondent has committed adultery and that the petitioner finds it intolerable to live with the respondent. If this is not done the petition will have to be amended and re-served.

6-16.3   It is no longer necessary to name the person with whom the adultery was committed – see FPR 2.7(1). It does not matter therefore whether the petitioner knows the name (but does not include it) or does not know the name (and cannot include it). The wording of the SP certificate should then be just 'the respondent's adultery'. In this case the petitioner will only be able to seek costs against the respondent.

6-16.4   It is poor practice to name a co-respondent unnecessarily, and it is now unusual to do so. It simply adds to costs, because another person has to be served. When a person is named, the petitioner's motivation is often to 'make a point' or attract notoriety. Where the person is named, he or she must be made a co-respondent and served with the petition in the same way as the respondent. If an order has been made for substituted service, check that the service requirements have been met.

6-16.5   Proof of adultery is usually now by way of admission in the acknowledgment of service (AOS). The signature of the respondent to the AOS will have to be verified by the petitioner (see under 'Service' later). If proof is by way of confession statement this will have to be verified, usually by the petitioner identifying the signature on the confession statement exhibited to the affidavit in support.

6-16.6   Without an admission by the respondent (and co-respondent, if joined), other cogent evidence will have to be provided. Evidence by the petitioner that the respondent 'admitted adultery' or what third parties have told the petitioner will not normally suffice.

6-16.7   If the only evidence against a co-respondent is the respondent's admission (in the AOS or confession statement) some district judges are reluctant to treat that as sufficient evidence of adultery against the co-respondent. However, under the Civil Evidence Act 1968, such evidence is admissible against the co-respondent.

---

[19]   MCA 1973 s 1(2); cf CPA 2004 s 44(5).

6-16.8   If there is insufficient evidence against the named co-respondent of adultery, the appropriate wording in the SP certificate is: 'the Respondent's adultery *with a (wo)man against whom the allegation is not proved'*.

6-16.9   If the petitioner and respondent have lived with each other in the same household for more than 6 months after the petitioner learned of the adultery, then the 'fact' of adultery cannot be relied on: s 2(1) MCA 1973. Of course, parties may live under the same roof, but not in the same household. However, clear evidence is needed that they were living apart if still under the same roof. Even if the 'fact' of adultery cannot then be relied on, the infidelity may still form part of a course of conduct showing unreasonable behaviour.

6-17   The 'Facts': Behaviour

6-17.1   The fact must be pleaded that 'the respondent has behaved in such a way that the petitioner cannot reasonably be expected to live with the respondent'. If this wording is not used the petition must be amended and re-served.

6-17.2   The behaviour may be positive or negative and may consist of specific incidents or a course of conduct.

6-17.3   This 'fact' is sometimes referred to as 'unreasonable behaviour'. This convenient shorthand is technically incorrect, because it suggests an objective standard. The wording of the statute (quoted above) provides a mainly subjective test.

6-17.4   The pleaded particulars of behaviour need not be unnecessarily antagonistic. But there does have to be some sufficient <u>behaviour by the respondent</u>. Some parties, in the bid to avoid controversy, produce anodyne particulars which do not meet the threshold (eg. 'the petitioner and respondent had many arguments and could not agree [about something]' or 'the petitioner and respondent had different expectations and lifestyles'). If the pleaded particulars are insufficient, then the petitioner should be allowed to provide more detail. This may be done by a further affidavit, but the respondent may need to be given notice of any amended allegations. Removal of the case from the special procedure list for hearing before a circuit judge in open court is very rare.

6-17.5   If the petitioner and respondent have lived with each other for more than 6 months after the last incident of behaviour relied upon, this is not a bar to relying on the 'fact' of behaviour, but the court may take it into account. This is the effect of s 2(3) of the MCA 1973. Most petitions include the phrase 'the behaviour is continuing' which generally avoids the difficulty. There is usually some good reason why the parties have continued to live together. Living together for up to six months is disregarded.

6-18   The 'Facts': Desertion

6-18.1   This is the least used of the 'facts'. Desertion requires the separation to be without the consent of the petitioner. Proof of this in the petitioner's affidavit in support is usually sufficient. An agreed separation is not desertion.

6-18.2   The period of two years must be completed before the date of the presentation of the petition. Periods of living together of up to six months do not break the overall separation but must be disregarded in calculating the two year period.

6-18.3   People may be separated even if living under the same roof, provided they are living in separate households. It is highly unlikely that desertion would be relied on in these circumstances. More likely it would then be a 'behaviour' or '2 years separation' petition.

6-18.4   The petitioner's affidavit in support of the petition must state the addresses of the parties throughout the period of separation. If it does not, the SP should be stopped and the affidavit returned so that the necessary details can be inserted and the affidavit re-sworn.

6-18.5   Beware: if the petition is amended to include desertion, the 2 year period must have expired before the date of filing of the original petition. This is because an amendment 'relates back' to the date of the original petition.

6-19   The 'Facts': Two Years' Separation and Consent

6-19.1   The period of two years must be completed before the date of the presentation of the petition. This period excludes the date of separation and the date of filing the petition. Having waited 2 years, some people file a day or two too soon. It is not the date of the petition which counts, but the date of filing (usually a few days later). This may be a crucial difference.

6-19.2   If the petition is amended to include this 'fact', the period must have expired before the date of the original petition. An amendment 'relates back' to the date of the original petition. Getting this wrong is a common error by practitioners.

6-19.3   Periods of living together of up to six months do not break the overall separation but must be disregarded in calculating the two year period. People may be separated even if living under the same roof, provided they are living in separate households.

6-19.4   Consent is usually proved by an answer to that effect in the AOS. The AOS must then be signed personally by the respondent (FPR 2.10). If the AOS includes such a signed consent, a copy of it is exhibited to the petitioner's affidavit in support, in which the petitioner verifies the signature of the respondent.

6-19.5   Sometimes a separate document signed by the respondent is relied on. The signature has to be verified in the same way. Generally, such a document should refer to the particular petition now brought (ie. be clearly produced in response to it, rather than signed before it was issued).

6-19.6   Occasionally a petitioner seeks to rely on a general consent, given pre-proceedings. This is not normally sufficient. This is because the two governing statutes require[20] that rules of court must be made:

---

[20]   MCA 1973 s 2(7); CPA 2004 s 45(4).

'for the purpose of ensuring that . . . the respondent has been given such information as will enable him to understand the consequences to him of his consenting to a decree being granted and the steps which he must take to indicate that he consents to the grant of a decree'.

The rules require that the respondent is sent a 'Notice of Proceedings' which contains this information,[21] together with the blank acknowledgment of service.

6-19.7   Silence is not consent. Do not therefore dispense with service of a petition under this head. An order for deemed service or substituted service will rarely be appropriate, unless the petitioner is also able to produce a written consent from the respondent (FPR 2.9(6A)).

6-19.8   If the respondent gives the court notice that he or she does not consent, or that a previous consent is withdrawn, the petition must be stayed unless a different 'fact' is also relied on: FPR 2.10(2).

6-20   The 'Facts': Five years' Separation

6-20.1   As with petitions based on desertion and 2 years' separation, the period of 5 years' separation must be completed before the date of filing of the petition (excluding the date of separation and date of filing). If the petition is amended to include this 'fact', the period must have expired before the date of the original petition.

6-20.2   Separation may be under the same roof, if there are separate households. Living together for up to 6 months does not prevent the period being continuous but the period of living together itself must not be counted as part of the five years.

6-21   The 'Prayer' for Relief

6-21.1   The prayer must state whether dissolution or judicial separation is sought.

6-21.2   A claim for costs may be included.

6-21.3   It is usual for a claim to be included for the various forms of financial orders ('ancillary relief' – see later).

6-22   Costs of the Dissolution or Separation Petition

6-22.1   Questions relating to claims for costs of the petition proceedings and decree or order frequently give rise to problems.

6-22.2   You may only make an order for the respondent to pay the costs if a claim for such costs is made in both the petition and the affidavit in support. If the claim is missing from either, you cannot order costs.

---

[21]   See FPR r 2.6(6) and Form M5 (matrimonial), or Form M5A (civil partnership).

6-22.3   If the claim is made in the petition but not in the affidavit in support, delete the claim in the SP certificate.

6-22.4   If the claim is missing from the petition, an amended petition is required before they can be properly claimed. Often the claim is missing from the petition, but is made later in the affidavit in support. This later claim is usually by oversight. Do not stop the SP on this ground alone. Simply delete the claim for costs in the SP certificate.

6-22.5   Check the AOS to see if the respondent has made any statement about costs.

6-22.6   If, as often occurs, the respondent objects in the AOS to paying the costs, then make a decision based on the information available to you, and complete the SP certificate accordingly. Whatever your decision on paper, the respondent has the right to be heard on the question of costs at the pronouncement of the decree (or partnership order).[22]

6-22.7   It is unhelpful to make an order that 'the question of costs shall be determined by the district judge on pronouncement of the decree'. That district judge will usually have less time and no more information than is available at the SP referral stage, and he or she will simply have to read the papers again. In the unlikely event that there is more information on the occasion of the pronouncement, this will only be because one or both parties attends court that day, or they have made further written representations. But the parties can do this in any event, so nothing is gained.

6-22.8   In practice most people accept the decision arrived at in the SP certificate. The costs of arguing over costs can be as large as the initial amount of the disputed costs.

6-22.9   Where there is a costs dispute many parties will accept a compromise that the respondent pays one half of the petitioner's costs, so that they are shared more or less equally. Both sides usually want the dissolution or separation order, and each would have had to pay the costs if they rather than the other person had petitioned.

6-23   *Acknowledgment of Service*

6-23.1   Service of the petition is usually proved by the respondent completing and returning to the court the AOS. If the respondent is acting in person the AOS is then exhibited to the petitioner's affidavit in support of the petition and the respondent's signature identified. If the AOS is signed by solicitors on behalf of the respondent, that is sufficient proof of service, and exhibiting a copy to the petitioner's affidavit may be unnecessary.

6-23.2   If the petitioner relies on the AOS for an admission of adultery or consent to a 2 year separation petition then the respondent must sign the AOS personally (even

---

[22]   FPR r 2.37.

if there are solicitors acting). The copy AOS must then be exhibited to the petitioner's affidavit in support, with the signature identified.

6-23.3 Check that the original AOS is on the court file. If it is not, stop the SP and ask that the original be filed. Sometimes it has been returned to the court but has not yet reached the file. Sometimes the respondent returns the AOS to the solicitors rather than the court, and it happens that the solicitors keep the original in their file and send in a photocopy. Always insist that the original is lodged before the SP certificate is signed.

6-24 Other Methods of Service

6-24.1 For more detail about service, go to the section 'Service of Petitions' *(see section 9 below)*.

6-25 Statement of Arrangements for Children

6-25.1 The 'statement of arrangements' must be signed personally by the petitioner, not the solicitors.[23] If the respondent has also signed it, or later submits a signed copy with the AOS, then the petitioner's affidavit in support of the petition should exhibit a copy of the page with that signature, and identify it.

6-25.2 At the time of the SP certificate, the court must 'consider':[24] whether there are any relevant children; and whether 'it should exercise any of its powers under the Children Act 1989 with respect to any of them'. Born of experience, we almost never now invoke those powers at the time of the SP certificate.

6-25.3 The relevant children are: 'children of the family' who are under 16 at the time of consideration; and children of the family who are 16 or 17 <u>and</u> in respect of whom the court gives an appropriate direction.

6-25.4 Some questions in the statement of arrangements may not be fully answered, but usually there is sufficient information overall. If necessary the SP can be stopped and further details requested, but this is rare.

6-25.5 The court does not have to certify that the arrangements are satisfactory (the test before 1991). If there is a disagreement between the parties about the arrangements, then either may make a free standing application under the Children Act. Experience shows that it is rarely of any benefit for the court itself to list a children appointment in response to the information in the statement of arrangements.

6-25.6 If one of the parties has already issued Children Act proceedings, then simply complete the part of the SP certificate which states whether there are children of the family, without anything more.

---

[23] FPR r 2.2(2) and Form M4.
[24] MCA 1973 s 41(1); CPA 2004 s 63.

6-25.7   If there are exceptional circumstances making it desirable 'in the interests of the children' to do so, the court may direct that the dissolution decree is not to be made absolute or the separation decree is not to be made, until the court orders otherwise. Almost by definition, it is extraordinary for a direction to be made holding up the decree in the interests of the children.

6-26   *The Special Procedure Certificate*

6-26.1   When completed, the certificate should make clear:

•   (matrimonial) whether the decree is for divorce or judicial separation (or, rarely, interim gender recognition nullity)

•   (civil partnership) whether the order is for dissolution or separation (or, rarely, interim gender recognition nullity)

•   (all cases) the 'fact'

•   (all cases) the costs order, if any

•   (all cases) whether or not there are relevant children of the family.

6-26.2   Strike though clearly those parts of the certificate which do not apply.

6-26.3   Fill out the certificate as far as possible, even if it is not completed and signed because of some outstanding query. This saves time by avoiding having to consider the same matters again later.

6-26.4   If you 'stop' the petition, complete the stop form concisely, and sign and date the stop. Make the stop message succinct, and sign and date it immediately under your message. Do not take up the whole box needlessly. Leave space underneath for any further stop. The same form can then be re-used. This saves the staff the job of writing out a further form later.

6-26.5   Place the stop form at the top of the file so that the staff do not think you have simply forgotten to sign the certificate.

6-27   *The Special Procedure Certificates in Consolidated Petitions*

6-27.1   Where there are consolidated petitions, completion of the SP certificates needs particular care. If the 'new style' technique for consolidation has been followed, the second petition will have become the cross petition and the second petitioner will be the respondent in the consolidated suit. *(See 'Order (New Style): Consolidation of Petitions and Title' para 7-06.4 below.)*

6-27.2   There should be 2 SP certificates, each headed identically with the same title as set out in the previous consolidation order, with both petition numbers in the title. Complete the 2 certificates by identifying the separate petition numbers in the body of the text (using the underlined italicised words, as follows):

(1)   For the petitioner, complete one certificate by inserting in the body text:

'The Petitioner has sufficiently proved the contents of the petition *No. FD09D01234* herein and is entitled to a decree ...' etc

(2)   For the respondent, complete the other certificate by inserting in the body text:

'The Respondent has sufficiently proved the contents of the *cross* petition *No. FD09D05678* herein and is entitled to a decree...' etc

6-28   *The SP Certificate and Consent Orders for Ancillary Relief*

6-28.1   Sometimes a consent financial application accompanies an SP application and the district judge both grants the SP certificate and approves the draft financial order.

6-28.2   Since this is before the decree is pronounced the financial ancillary relief order cannot be made at the time of the SP referral. You should therefore mark the financial consent application 'approved subject to decree' and sign and date it. Do not purport to make an order on the ancillary relief application – it is a nullity before the decree.

6-28.3   The pre-printed blank certificate includes a section to make an agreed financial order (ancillary relief) at the same time as the pronouncement of the decree.

6-28.4   If the proposed financial order is appropriate, the district judge's certificate should be completed by including in the appropriate box the words:

Direction: SP Certificate with Ancillary Relief

". . . and to an order for ancillary relief as agreed between the petitioner and respondent in the terms approved by the court on *{date}*"

(or similarly identifying it)

6-28.5   If such an order is proposed, the documents which must be sent with the SP affidavit are (the originals of):

* the draft order, signed by both parties (or their solicitors, if they are on the record)

* any necessary annex (eg. pension sharing)

* statements of financial information (Form D81, previously M1)

* Forms A for both parties

6-28.6   If the draft financial order is not acceptable, do not stop the SP certificate. Complete the other parts of the SP certificate and sign it. List the queries about the financial draft on the back of the draft financial order. Those matters can be dealt with later after the decree has been pronounced.

6-28.7   Sometimes the financial consent application comes up for consideration between the signing of the district judge's SP certificate and the pronouncement of decree.

6-28.8   The certificate will then appear with the ancillary relief box deleted rather than completed. If the agreed terms are approved, it is generally preferable for any amendment to the SP certificate to be by the district judge who originally signed the certificate.[25] In these circumstances, it may be better for a deputy district judge to refer that aspect of the case to a full-time district judge.

6-28.9   For further guidance about financial orders, see:

- *section 10 below –'Financial Claims: Ancillary Relief'*

- in particular *paras 10-27 to 10-34 below* – '*Consent Orders* – *General Matters'*

---

[25]   Secretary's Circular 24 November 1977: Amendment of District Judge's Certificate – Family Division Directions p C5.

7 Supplemental, Amended, Consolidated and Cross-Petitions

7-01 Introduction

7-01.1 A variety of problems may arise when dealing with cases where there are supplemental or amended petitions (and with consolidated or cross-petitions – see later). Misunderstandings about them are the source of many (un)happy hours of work for both practitioners and district judges.

7-02 Supplemental Petitions

7-02.1 Distinguish a supplemental petition from an amended petition.

7-02.2 A supplemental petition is not a new petition, it supplements the existing one. It is used to add new factual particulars arising since the original petition and in support of the existing 'fact' already relied on. A supplemental petition cannot therefore be used to add a new 'fact' (ie. the basis for dissolution or separation).

7-02.3 A supplemental petition may be filed without leave at any time before an answer is filed or (if there is no answer) before 'directions for trial' have been given. After that, leave is required.[1] (For *'Directions for Trial' – see para 5-01 above.*)

7-02.4 Supplemental petitions are rare these days. Classically, they were used to add further particulars of behaviour in defended suits where the petitioner wished to 'beef up' the original particulars with later allegations for the contested hearing.

7-02.5 They may still be used where the parties attempt a reconciliation after the issue of the original petition, the reconciliation fails and the petitioner wishes to add further subsequent particulars to show irretrievable breakdown despite the reconciliation.

7-02.6 A supplemental petition must be served in the normal way, with proof of service. The affidavit in support of the petition should refer also to the supplemental petition.

7-03 Amended Petitions

7-03.1 An amended petition is used to add matters which existed at the date of the original petition, but were omitted or need correction.

7-03.2 If the petitioner wishes to add another 'fact' which existed at the date of the original petition that may be done by an amended petition.

7-03.3 The amendment 'relates back' to the date of the original petition, ie. it is treated as though the amendment was always there.

---

[1] FPR rr 2.11(1), 2.14 and 2.18(1).

7-03.4   The petitioner cannot amend a petition to rely on a new 'fact' arising since the filing of the original petition; that must be done by issuing a new petition. Note the restrictions about 2 petitions. *(See: 'Two Concurrent Petitions' para 7-04 below.)*

7-03.5   A common error by practitioners is to try to amend a petition based on behaviour to add '2 years separation', when the period of separation was not long enough at the date of the original petition, but is by the date of the amendment. Another error is to amend to allege adultery which first occurred after the filing of the original petition. Neither is allowed. The 'fact' must have existed at the original date.

7-03.6   An amended petition may be filed without leave at any time before an answer is filed or (if there is no answer) before directions for trial have been given. After that, any amendment requires leave.[2] (*See 'Directions for Trial' para 5-01 above.*)

7-04   *Two Concurrent Petitions*

7-04.1   A petitioner cannot usually present another concurrent petition in respect of the same marriage or partnership unless the court gives leave.[3] This does not prevent the respondent from filing his or her own first petition, without leave.

7-04.2   If therefore the petitioner wishes to issue a new petition, this requires the dismissal of the existing petition, or leave to issue a second concurrent petition even though the first petition has not been dismissed. *(See: the Specimen Order at para 6-13.8 above)*

7-04.3   Where 2 parties have each issued their own petition, they frequently agree to proceed on one petition only. This is the least complicated solution. Usually the other petitioner wishes to be sure that the other party will proceed with the agreed petition before abandoning their own. Once the decree nisi (conditional order) has been pronounced in the agreed petition, the respondent can obtain the decree absolute (final order) by applying in that petition. The following order achieves this (assuming no Answer has been filed in either).

> Order: Proceed on one Petition and Stay the other
>
> On the Petitioner and Respondent agreeing to proceed under the Special Procedure in Petition No. FD09D01234 as an undefended suit
>
> ORDER
> Petition No. FD09D05678 is stayed until further order, and shall be dismissed on the pronouncement of the decree in Petition No. FD09D01234

7-04.4   If ancillary relief applications have already been issued, check whether you are dismissing the petition in which those claims are being made. If appropriate,

---

[2]   FPR rr 2.11(1), 2.14 and 2.18(1).
[3]   FPR rr 2.6(4) and 2.6(4A).

make an order in the continuing petition that any existing ancillary relief documents and orders in the other petition are treated as filed and made in the continuing petition.

7-05   *Consolidation of Petitions*

7-05.1   Where there are 2 concurrent opposing petitions (one each by the 2 parties) and both wish to continue with their respective petitions, then the 2 petitions should be consolidated.

7-05.2   Where one petition is for separation and the other is for divorce, then the divorce decree effectively makes the separation decree otiose. A stay of the separation petition and proceeding on the divorce petition may be a more practical solution.

7-05.3   It is important that all the proceedings affecting the validity of the marriage or partnership be coordinated. This avoids a 'petition race', where one party seeks to get 'their' final order first. A marriage or civil partnership can only be dissolved once, so there can only ever be one decree absolute (final order). If the petitions are consolidated the single decree absolute will properly refer to both the petitioner's and respondent's grounds for divorce. This way both parties obtain a decree absolute on the facts of 'their own' petition.

7-06   *Consolidation of Petitions: Title of Proceedings*

7-06.1   When petitions are consolidated the title of the proceedings becomes problematic. The long standing practice has been to make appropriate orders in both suits, identifying the 'lead suit' and giving the consolidated suit the title as follows:

Title (Old Style): Consolidation of Petitions and Title

[Court]		
Nos:	FD09D01234	
	FD09D05678	
Between	Amanda Ankle	Wife
and	Barry Bruiser	Husband
and	Coleen Crumpet	Co-Respondent
	and	
Between	Barry Bruiser	Husband
and	Amanda Ankle	Wife

7-06.2   This form of title is now inappropriate, both in matrimonial petitions since the Gender Recognition Act President's Direction *(see para 6-02 above)*, and in civil partnership petitions. 'Husband' and 'wife' must no longer be used in the title or orders in matrimonial cases, and of course cannot be used in civil partnerships. A consistent practice for both types of petitions is needed. A complete rethink is called for.

7-06.3   The petition which is earliest in time is usually chosen as the lead petition in the consolidated suit. The title should also identify parties in a way which can be used conveniently in later orders, especially ancillary relief.

7-06.4   The solution agreed by district judges in the Principal Registry is that the following order and form of title be used. This order must be made in both petitions before consolidation.

Order (New Style): Consolidation of Petitions and Title

ORDER
1.   Petitions FD09D01234 and FD09D05678 be consolidated.
2.   Petition FD09D01234 be the lead petition, and petition FD09D05678 be treated as a cross petition.
3.   The title of the consolidated suit shall be:

[Court]
Nos: FD09D01234
               FD09D05678
In the consolidated Cross Petitions
Between   Amanda Ankle   Petitioner
and   Barry Bruiser   Respondent
and   Coleen Crumpet   Co-Respondent

8 **Resolving Defended Petitions or Cross Petitions**

8-01 Answers and Cross-Petitions

8-01.1 Sometimes a respondent just denies the allegations in the petition and asks that it be dismissed. This is a simple Answer.

8-01.2 More commonly, a respondent files an Answer which defends the petition and also seeks a decree, dissolution or separation order for him or herself. This is an Answer and Cross-Petition. Strictly, the part which denies the allegations in the petition is the Answer, and the part which claims a decree or order is the Cross-Petition. Each part should have a separate heading, but this is commonly neglected. The petitioner should then file and serve a Reply if the intention is to defend the Cross-Petition. Both the petition and cross-petition then become defended, and the Special Procedure cannot be used for either.

8-01.3 To avoid a (public) trial and unnecessary legal costs, it is common for the parties later to agree to proceed with an undefended suit under the special procedure. This is done in one of 5 ways:

(1) to strike out the Answer and Cross-Petition, and proceed on the undefended petition. (This is the simplest and usual method);

(2) to proceed on the undefended Answer and Cross-Petition;

(3) to proceed by undefended cross-petitions;

(4) to amend the petition, and then proceed on the undefended amended petition;

(5) to proceed on a new petition on a different fact, and stay the current petition and answer.

8-01.4 These techniques can be used either to resolve the defended suit where an Answer or Cross-Petition has been filed or (with necessary modifications) to avoid disputes before the suit has become defended.

8-02 Striking Out the Answer and Cross-Petition

8-02.1 If the Answer and Cross-Petition are struck out, the suit can proceed undefended on the original petition. This is the simplest and usual method.

Order: Striking Out Answer and Cross-Petition

[Recital, if needed]

The respondent reserves the right to dispute any factual matters set out in the particulars of behaviour in the petition should they be relevant in any subsequent applications

ORDER
1.   The Answer and Cross-Petition are struck out.
2.   The suit is to proceed undefended on the Petition under the Special Procedure

8-02.2   The result is that, in effect, the Answer and Cross-Petition cease to exist (though the documents remain on the court file).

8-03   *An Undefended Answer and Cross-Petition*

8-03.1   The parties may choose to proceed only on the Answer and Cross-Petition (strictly speaking, only on the Cross-Petition – *see para 8-01.2 above*). The order to achieve this requires some care in drafting. It is incorrect simply to dismiss the petition, because the Answer and Cross-Petition depend for their existence on the court file which includes the petition. Equally, it is inapt to 'dismiss the prayer in the petition', because the prayer usually contains the financial claims which must be retained. It is only the 'prayer for dissolution (or separation)' which should be affected. The right technique is illustrated below.

Order: Proceeding on Undefended Answer and Cross Petition

[Recital, if needed]
The petitioner reserves the right to dispute any factual matters set out in the particulars of behaviour in the [Answer and] Cross-Petition should they be relevant in any subsequent applications

ORDER
1.   The prayer for dissolution in the Petition be stayed forthwith and dismissed on the pronouncement of the decree in the [Answer and] Cross Petition.
2.   The suit is to proceed undefended on the [Answer and] Cross-Petition under the Special Procedure

8-04   *Undefended Cross-Petitions*

8-04.1   This situation shows the value of proper pleading, with an Answer and Cross-Petition headed in separate parts. If pleaded properly, the Answer can then be struck out, leaving the Cross-Petition intact, and ordering undefended decrees on the Petition and Cross-Petition. Sadly, this correct pleading is largely a lost art, so more detail must be included in any order. What must be struck out are the parts of the Answer which deny the allegations in the Petition, leaving in place the parts which assert a positive case in support of the Cross-Petition for dissolution or separation.

Order: Proceeding on Undefended Cross-Petitions

ORDER
1.   Paragraphs [n1, n2, n3 etc] of the Answer are struck out.

2.   The suit is to proceed by undefended cross decrees on the Petition and the [Answer and] Cross-Petition under the Special Procedure

8-04.2   Where 2 petitions have been consolidated *(see para 7-06.4 above)* there may be no Answer to strike out. For clarity, it may be clearer to insert the individual numbers of the 2 petitions in the above paragraph.

8-05   An Undefended Amended Petition

8-05.1   Often a respondent disputes some particulars in the petition but will accept a modified version (typically, less serious behaviour or adultery after separation rather than before). This may be dealt with either by amending the petition or by the petitioner agreeing to rely on some only of the pleaded particulars.

Order: Proceeding on an Amended Petition

ORDER
1.   The Petitioner may amend the petition [in the form attached to this order] [without re-service].
2.   On filing the amended petition the Answer [and Cross Petition] is struck out and the suit is to proceed undefended on the amended petition under the Special Procedure.

Order: Proceeding on Some Only of the Particulars

ORDER
1.   The Petition is to proceed under the Special Procedure on terms that the petitioner relies only on paragraphs [n1, n3, n4, n7, and n8] of the particulars [of behaviour].

8-06   A New Petition on a Different Fact

8-06.1   If the parties agree to proceed on a new 'fact' (typically 2 years' separation or adultery, rather than an existing disputed behaviour petition), then the appropriate technique is:

Order: New Petition on a Different Fact

On the petitioner and respondent agreeing to proceed by a new petition based on [2 years' separation] under the special procedure

ORDER
1.   The Petitioner [Respondent] may issue a new petition based on [2 years' separation] even though the petition and cross petition in file no. FD09D01234 have not been disposed of
2.   The petition and cross petition in file no. FD0901234 be stayed on

the issue of the new petition and dismissed on the pronouncement of the decree in the new petition.

8-06.2   If a new petition is issued, check that an order is made in the new petition that any existing ancillary relief documents and orders are treated as filed and made in the new petition.

9   Service of Petitions

9-01   *Petitions: Service – General Matters*

9-01.1   The modes of service of a petition are prescribed in FPR r 2.9. The normal methods are by personal service or by post.

9-01.2   The petitioner is not allowed to effect personal service of the petition.[1]

9-01.3   It is not realistic to require a solicitor giving publicly funded 'Legal Help' to undertake extensive (and expensive) enquiries as to the whereabouts of the respondent.

9-02   *Petitions: Other Provisions as to Service*

9-02.1   The following are some of the other main rules relating to service:

- Service on a child or protected party[2] [FPR r 9.3].

- Service on solicitors [FPR r 10.2].

- Service on person acting in person [FPR r 10.3].

- Dispensing with service on person acting in person [FPR r 10.3(3)].

- Bailiff service [FPR rr 2.9(4) and (10); r 10.4].

- Proof of service by officer of court [FPR r 10.5].

- Substituted service [FPR r 2.9(9) – petitions; FPR r 10.2(1) and r 10.3(1) – generally].

- Service by advertisement [FPR r 2.9(9) – petitions; FPR r 10.5(3) – generally].

- Service out of England and Wales [FPR r 10.6].

- Application of County Court Rules and Rules of the Supreme Court [FPR r 1.3 – CCR and RSC apply to family proceedings subject to the modifications in the FPR].

- CCR Ord 7 rr 1, 3 and 8 – service within the jurisdiction.

- CCR Ord 8 – service out of England and Wales.

- RSC Ord 10 – service of originating process within jurisdiction.

---

[1]   FPR r 2.9(3).
[2]   Someone who lacks capacity under the Mental Health Act 2005: FPR r 9.1(1).

- RSC Ord 11 – service of originating process out of jurisdiction.

- RSC Ord 65 – service of documents.

9-03   *Proof of Service by Officer of the Court*

9-03.1   Where a petition is sent to any person by an officer of the court, he shall note the date of posting in the records of the court. This court record is evidence of the facts stated in it.[3] Of course, in the absence of an AOS or further information, the fact of posting does not of itself prove that the Respondent has received the petition.

9-04   *Affidavit of Service*

9-04.1   Where the petition is served on the respondent personally (usually by a process server), the affidavit of service must state how the server has identified the respondent. Commonly, the affidavit gives a time, date and place of service and says 'the respondent admitted his(her) identity to me'. This is often treated as sufficient. Arguably, it is inadequate, because an admission of identity does not prove that the person is who they say they are. A better method is by a photograph (exhibited to the affidavit). Sometimes the petitioner may point out the respondent to the process server.

9-04.2   Check that there is a complete 'chain of proof' about service. Where identification is by photograph, the process server's affidavit should exhibit the photograph and an affidavit from the petitioner (usually the SP affidavit) should also identify that photograph or exhibit a further copy of it. Similarly, where the petitioner has pointed out the respondent, both the affidavit of the server and that of the petitioner should say so.

9-05   *Bailiff Service*

9-05.1   A party may request bailiff service.[4] This needs a direction by a district judge. Such a request should be made only if the signed AOS is not returned to the court after normal service by post. Bailiff service is not normally directed unless the party is a litigant in person. Where a solicitor is acting, the solicitor must show why bailiff service is required, instead of personal service by a process server.

9-05.2   The bailiff returns a certificate to show whether, and if so, when and how service was effected. The petitioner may provide a photograph to identify the respondent, which is then returned to the court with the bailiff's certificate.

---

[3]   FPR r 10.5; s 133 County Courts Act 1984.
[4]   FPR rr 2.9(4) and 10.4; see also Family Division Directions p C2-C3.

9-05.3   Check the 'chain of proof' about service *(see para 9-04.2 above)*. Frequently a bailiff will obtain the respondent's signature, which should then be identified by the petitioner in the affidavit in support.

9-06   *Petitions: Deemed Service*

9-06.1   Service may be deemed where the district judge is satisfied that the petition has been received by the respondent but no acknowledgement of service has been filed.[5]

9-07   *Petitions: Deemed Service – The Armed Forces*

9-07.1   For a member of HM Forces, service can be effected on the person's commanding officer.[6]

9-08   *Petitions: Substituted Service*

9-08.1   Do not order substituted service unless you are satisfied the process is likely to reach the respondent.

9-08.2   A common form of substituted service is by posting or delivering the document to the respondent c/o the address of a family member known to be in touch with or visited by the respondent.

> Order: Substituted Service
>
> Until further order, documents including orders in these proceedings may be served on the Respondent by placing them in a sealed envelope addressed to the Respondent and sent by first class pre-paid post 'c/o {address}', and service shall be deemed to be effected [7] days after such posting.

9-08.3   Service by advertisement is for practical purposes not used.

9-09   *Petitions: Letter Forwarding*

9-09.1   In the past the Department of Social Security was prepared to forward one letter to the address of the respondent last known to the department. In the absence of an acknowledgement of service, forwarding the petition in this way did not prove service. Sufficient identifying details for the respondent had to be given.

9-09.2   This service is now withdrawn. In any event, the Department of Social Security no longer exists. Its functions have been taken over by HM Revenue and Customs (HMRC) and the Department for Work and Pensions (DWP).

---

[5]   FPR r 2.9(6).

[6]   Section 62 Armed Forces Act 1971, which amends: s 101 Naval Act 1957; s 153 Army Act 1955; s 153 Air Force Act 1955.

9-10   *Petitions: Dispensing with Service*

9-10.1   Where it is impracticable to serve a party or it is otherwise necessary or expedient to dispense with service of the petition on the respondent or on any other person the district judge may make an order dispensing with such service [FPR r 2.9(11)].

9-10.2   Do not dispense with service of a petition based on the fact of 2 years' separation and consent[7] as this usually makes consent impossible to prove.

9-10.3   An application to dispense with service of the petition must be by affidavit. There is no separate notice of application.[8]

9-10.4   The standard form affidavit is generally used.[9]

9-10.5   The notes of guidance with the standard affidavit state that if the respondent has not been heard of for 2 years or more, the affidavit should exhibit or be accompanied by the result of a decree absolute search, to ensure that the respondent has not already divorced the petitioner. Most district judges however require a decree absolute search after a lapse of only a year or to cover the period from the date of separation to the date of the petition.

9-10.6   It is generally not satisfactory for the affidavit to state that nothing is known of the respondent, and no enquiries can or have been made. In such a case a more detailed explanation should be called for from the petitioner as to why so little is known of the respondent.

9-10.7   A decree absolute/partnership final order search (where appropriate) and a full explanation of why service cannot be attempted via an address of a family member or friend are common minimum requirements before dispensing with service of the petition.

9-10.8   Sometimes however dispensing with service is not what is required.

9-11   *Petitions: Addresses from Government Departments*

9-11.1   There is a 1989 Registrar's Direction[10] which sets out the circumstances in which the <u>court</u> was able to request disclosure of addresses by government departments. It is still in force, but its value is now very depleted. It must be treated with caution, and the details of contact addresses may no longer be accurate. Disclosure of addresses from some government departments is subject to newer protocols and guidance from the President's office and more recent departmental and statutory changes.

---

7   MCA 1973 s 1(2)(d) or CPA 2004 s 44(5)(b).
8   FPR r 2.9(11).
9   Practice Direction 7 March 1977, para 8. Family Division Directions pp C2-3.
10   See Registrar's Direction 13 February 1989 – Family Division Directions pp A13-16. Set out in full in *Rayden & Jackson on Divorce and Family Matters*, Vol 1(2) para 55.120. See also [1988] 1 WLR 648.

9-11.2   Despite those changes, the 1989 Direction would still apply to the service of petitions (provided they contain a prayer for financial ancillary relief) and to service of proceedings for financial provision orders.

9-11.3   But for practical purposes, the 1989 Direction is of little value for the service of petitions with, or proceedings for, financial claims. This is because National Insurance records (the main source to trace adults) are no longer held by the Department for Work and Pensions (previously the Department of Social Security). These records are now held by HM Revenue and Customs, which has a statutory duty of confidentiality.

9-11.4   HM Revenue and Customs will only disclose an address if a High Court inherent jurisdiction order is made under the President's Guidance 2003.

9-11.5   For a more general and fuller treatment of disclosure of addresses see the later sections of these notes under:

- *Disclosure of Addresses and Information from Non Parties (see para 18 below)*

- *Disclosure of Information: Government Departments – The Registrar's Direction 1989 (see para 18-06 below)*

9.11.6   *Table 5: Government Departments – Addresses and Requirements (see para 18-09 below)* gives current details of contact addresses and a summary of the circumstances in which, and the method by which, disclosure may be sought, as well as a guide to the forms of orders to be used. There are specimen orders at the end of these notes.

10   Financial Claims: 'Ancillary Relief'

10-01   Introduction

10-01.1   Not all financial claims heard in the context of family proceedings are 'ancillary relief' applications.

10-01.2   **'Ancillary relief' is a term of art under the FPR rules**. It means:[1]

(1)   an avoidance of disposition order

(2)   a financial provision order (which includes pension attachment)

(3)   an order for maintenance pending suit

(4)   an order for maintenance pending outcome of proceedings

(5)   a property adjustment order

(6)   a variation order

(7)   a pension sharing order

10-01.3   These descriptions apply to some only of the orders made under Part II of the Matrimonial Causes Act 1973 and section 72(1) and Schedule 5 of the Civil Partnership Act 2004.

10-01.4   This has important procedural consequences, including which costs rules apply. Notably, the costs rules have changed for ancillary relief applications made from 3 April 2006.

10-02   Financial Claims which are not 'Ancillary Relief'

10-02.1   The principal classes of family financial claims which are not 'ancillary relief' are as follows (see the later individual sections for a brief treatment):

•   Children Act 1989: Schedule 1

•   Transfer of Tenancies: Schedule 7 of the Family Law Act 1996

•   Inheritance (Provision for Family and Dependants) Act 1975

•   Trusts of Land and Appointment of Trustees Act 1996

•   Failure to Maintain: Marriage and Civil Partnership

•   Financial Relief after Foreign Divorce/Dissolution

---

[1]   FPR r 1.2(1).

10-03   Marriage/Partnership: Home Rights

10-03.1   'Matrimonial home rights' are (since 5 December 2005) now called 'home rights' and apply equally to marriage and civil partnership.[2]

10-04   Marriage and Civil Partnership: Financial Claims Compared

10-04.1   The intention expressed in the Civil Partnership Act 2004 is to make 'provision for financial relief in connection with civil partnerships that corresponds to provision made for financial relief in connection with marriages'.[3]

10-05   Substantive Orders – General

10-05.1   Under the Matrimonial Causes Act 1973 and the Civil Partnership Act 2004 the court has jurisdiction to make only the substantive orders set out in the relevant statutes. Table 3 *(para 10-07 below)* summarises those classes of orders, and compares the relevant sections under the 1973 and 2004 Acts.

10-05.2   Note, for example, that there is no power to order that a party be responsible for debts, or pay insurance premium payments.

10-06   Substantive Orders – Descriptions

10-06.1   Orders under s 23 MCA 1973 and Sch 5 Part 1 CPA 2004 for periodical payments, secured periodical payments and lump sums (as supplemented by pension attachment orders) are defined as 'financial provision orders'.[4]

10-06.2   Pension attachment orders are also 'financial provision orders'. This is because they are made under s 25B and 25C MCA 1973 and Sch 5 Part 6 para 25 and 26 CPA 2004, which are supplementary powers to orders under (respectively) s 23 MCA 1973 and Sch 5 Part 1 CPA 2004.

10-06.3   Orders under s 24 MCA 1973 and Sch 5 Part 2 CPA 2004 for the transfer of property, settlement of property or variation of settlements are all 'property adjustment orders'.[5]

10-06.4   Orders under s 24B MCA 1973 and Sch 5 Part 4 CPA 2004 are all 'pension sharing orders'.[6]

10-06.5   The generic descriptions can therefore be accurately and economically used in orders – eg. 'all claims for financial provision, property adjustment and pension sharing orders for either party be dismissed'.

---

[2]   Section 30 Family Law Act 1996 was amended by Sch 9 CPA 2004.
[3]   See generally: s 72(1) and Sch 5 CPA 2004 and FPR r 1.2(1).
[4]   Section 21(1) MCA 1973 and s 72 and heading to Sch 5 Part 1 CPA 2004.
[5]   S 21(2) MCA 1973 and Sch 5 Part 2 CPA 2004.
[6]   S 21A(1) MCA 1973 and Sch 5 Part 4 CPA 2004.

10-06.6   Orders under s 31 MCA 1973 and Sch 5 Part 11 CPA 2004 are all referred to as 'variation orders'.[7]

10-07   *Table 3: Ancillary Relief – Matrimonial/Civil Partnership Compared*

	Matrimonial	**Civil Partnership**
Orders	**MCA 1973**	**CPA 2004**
maintenance pending suit/outcome	s 22	Sch 5 Part 8 para 38
financial provision	s 23	Sch 5 Part 1 para 1
property adjustment	s 24	Sch 5 Part 2 para 6
sale	s 24A	Sch 5 Part 3 para 10
pension sharing	s 24B (petitions from 1.12.2000)	Sch 5 Part 4 para 15
pension attachment	s 25B and 25C (petitions from 1.7.1996)	Sch 5 Part 6 para 25 and 26
variation order	s 31	Sch 5 Part 11 para 51
lump sum and property adjustment on variation	s 31(7B) but only supplemental to and on discharge or termination of periodical payments	Sch 5 Part 11 para 53 but only supplemental to and on discharge or termination of periodical payments
avoidance of disposition/ transaction	s 37	Sch 5 Part 14 para 74

10-08   *Orders: Jurisdiction and Effective Dates*

10-08.1   Most of the substantive orders for financial ancillary relief can only be made on or after a matrimonial decree has been granted or a civil partnership (CP) order made on the petition. The exceptions are:

(1)   avoidance of disposition/transaction;

(2)   maintenance pending suit/outcome;

---

[7]   FPR r 1.2(1).

(3) 'financial provision' for children.

10-08.2   If other substantive financial orders are purportedly made before a decree or CP order they are a nullity (see later).

10-08.3   There are other limitations on the making of some financial orders. There are also restrictions on the date when some financial orders can be brought into effect.

10-08.4   *Table 4: Ancillary Relief – Jurisdiction and Effective Dates (see para 10-09 below)* summarises the main types of ancillary relief orders, the type of proceedings in which they may be made and at what stage in those proceedings, and the earliest dates when the differing orders may take effect.

10-08.5   In a petition for judicial separation (matrimonial) or a civil partnership separation order the 'cause' is determined by a single decree or CP order. In those petitions for separation the available substantive ancillary orders are more limited, but can be made and are effective immediately on decree (or CP order). Importantly, pension sharing orders cannot be made in such petitions.

10-08.6   In a petition for divorce, civil partnership (CP) dissolution, and nullity the 'cause' is determined in two stages – a decree nisi (or CP conditional order) followed by a later decree absolute (or CP final order). In those petitions the full range of substantive ancillary relief orders are available and can be made on decree nisi (or CP conditional order) but are not effective until the decree absolute (or CP final order).

10-08.7   An order for financial provision, property adjustment or pension sharing for a spouse/civil partner, or a property adjustment order for a child, made before the decree nisi, conditional partnership order, judicial separation or civil partnership separation order is a nullity.[8]

10-08.8   Financial provision orders for children <u>can</u> be made and take effect before decree/partnership order.[9]

10-08.9   But property adjustment orders for children and spousal/partner orders for financial provision, property adjustment and pension sharing <u>cannot</u> be made before decree/partnership order, <u>but can</u> be made on or after decree/order and do <u>not take effect</u> until decree absolute/final order.[10]

10-08.10   Any spousal/partner order for financial provision, property adjustment or pension sharing, and any child order for property adjustment, made on or after decree nisi/conditional order but before decree absolute/final order should be expressed to be 'subject to decree absolute/final order'.

10-08.11   See *Table 4: Ancillary Relief – Jurisdiction and Effective Dates (para 10-09 below)*.

---

8   *Board v Checkland* [1987] 2 FLR 257.
9   Section 23(2)(a) MCA 1973 and Sch 5 Part 1 para 1(2) CPA 2004.
10   See ss 23(5) and 24(3) MCA 1973 and Sch 5 Part 1 para 1(1) CPA 2004.

10-09   *Table 4: Ancillary Relief – Jurisdiction and Effective Dates*

Type of Order	Jurisdiction Arises (on or after)	Takes Effect
maintenance pending suit/outcome	divorce/dissolution/nullity: – petition	on financial order, until – decree absolute – CP final order
	separation: – petition	on financial order, until – JS decree – CP separation order
financial provision – child	divorce/dissolution/nullity: – petition – dismissal of petition after start of trial – within reasonable period after such dismissal	on financial order on financial order on financial order
	separation – petition – dismissal of petition after start of trial – within reasonable period after such dismissal	on financial order on financial order on financial order
financial provision – adult **property adjustment – adult** **property adjustment – child**	divorce/dissolution/nullity: – divorce/nullity decree nisi – CP conditional order	on decree absolute on CP final order
	separation: – judicial separation decree – CP separation order	on JS decree on CP separation order
pension sharing – adult	divorce/dissolution/nullity: – divorce/nullity decree nisi (petitions from 1.12.2000) – CP conditional order	on decree absolute on CP final order
	separation: (not available)	—
pension attachment – adult	divorce/dissolution/nullity: – divorce/nullity decree nisi (petitions from 1.7.1996) – CP conditional order	on decree absolute on CP final order
	separation: – judicial separation decree (petitions from 1.7.1996) – CP separation order	on JS decree on CP separation order

Type of Order	Jurisdiction Arises (on or after)	Takes Effect
sale of property **– s 24A MCA 1973** **– Sch 5 Part 3 CPA 2004**	divorce/dissolution/nullity: – divorce/nullity decree nisi – CP conditional order *but only with or after an order for:* – *secured periodical payments* – *lump sum* – *property adjustment*	on decree absolute on CP final order
	separation: – judicial separation decree – CP separation order *but only with an order for:* – *secured periodical payments* – *lump sum* – *property adjustment*	on JS decree on CP separation order
sale of land **– FPR r 2.64(3)**	with 'ancillary relief': – ancillary relief application	on order for sale
lump sum, property adjustment and pension sharing on variation	divorce/dissolution: – divorce decree nisi – CP conditional order *but only supplemental to and on discharge or termination of periodical payments*	on decree absolute on CP final order
	nullity: – (not available)	—
	separation: – (not available, except limited property adjustment on rescission)	—
avoidance of disposition/transaction	divorce/dissolution/nullity/ separation: – financial relief proceedings	on order

10-10 *Pension Claims – Jurisdiction*

10-10.1   Distinguish:

- **pension sharing** orders (s 24B MCA 1973 and Sch 5 Part 4 CPA 2004); from

- **pension attachment** orders (ss 25B and 25C MCA 1973 and Sch 5 Part 6 CPA 2004).

10-10.2   Pension sharing orders are a separate class of order. Pension attachment orders are a species of 'financial provision' orders.

10-10.3   Pension sharing is not available in a judicial separation or civil partnership separation petition.

10-10.4   Spousal pension sharing orders can be made only in a divorce or nullity petition filed on or after 1 December 2000.[11] Even where there is a cross petition, it is the date of the original petition which is relevant.[12]

10-10.5   Beware therefore, if a non-qualifying spousal petition is consolidated with a later qualifying respondent's petition, the respondent may lose the right to claim pension sharing.

10-10.6   Spousal pension attachment orders (formerly known as 'earmarking' orders) can only in be made divorce, nullity and judicial separation petitions filed on or after 1 July 1996.

10-10.7   Both pension attachment and pension sharing orders can be made in spousal petitions for divorce or nullity filed since 1 December 2000. But only one type of order can be made in respect of each pension arrangement (between the same parties and in the same marriage).

10-10.8   Claims for pension sharing and pension attachment orders in civil partnership petitions follow the same rules as spousal petitions. The date for all civil partnerships petitions falls, of course, after the 2 qualifying dates.

10-11   *Sale of Property – Jurisdiction*

10-11.1   The court has power to order the sale of property and a wide power to include directions on such sale.

10-11.2   The power to order sale under s 24A MCA 1973 and Sch 5 Part 3 para 10 CPA 2004 is exercisable over any property of the parties, but only on or after making a lump sum, property adjustment order or secured periodical payments order (ie. only on or after decree nisi and taking effect only on decree absolute). When making such an order for sale, the court may include in the order 'such consequential or supplementary provisions as the court thinks fit'.[13]

10-11.3   But there is a wider power to order sale of <u>land</u> available under RSC Ord 31 r 1 (applied to ancillary relief applications by FPR r 2.64(3)). It is exercisable <u>at any time</u>, before or after decree/partnership order, where 'it appears necessary or expedient' that the land be sold. The court may then 'give such directions as it thinks fit for the purpose of effecting the sale' including requiring payment of the purchase money 'to trustees or other persons'.[14]

10-11.4   (See also *'Pension Claims – Procedure and the Order' – para 10-30 below*).

---

[11]   Welfare Reform and Pensions Act 1999, Sch 4, para 1; and SI 2000/1116.
[12]   *W v W* [2002] 2 FLR 1225.
[13]   Section 24A(2) MCA 1973 and Sch 5 Part 3 para 11(2) CPA 2004.
[14]   RSC Ord 31 r 2(2).

10-12   Ancillary Relief: The Rules

10-12.1   As already stated, 'ancillary relief' is a term of art under the FPR rules.[15] This has important procedural consequences, and affects the costs rules which apply, particularly with ancillary relief applications made from 3 April 2006. (See *'The Costs Rules' – para 10-13 below*).

10-12.2   The specific rules relating to financial 'ancillary relief' (FAR) applications appear at FPR rr 2.51B–2.70.[16]

10-12.3   Any FAR application by a petitioner, or by a respondent who files an answer claiming relief, must be made in the petition or answer.[17]

10-12.4   Check the petition (answer) to see if FAR claims have been made.

10-12.5   An answer which defends without a cross prayer is not 'an answer claiming relief'.

10-12.6   An answer which is struck out ceases to exist though the document remains on file.

10-12.7   In most cases (undefended petitions) the petition will contain financial claims.

10-12.8   If the claims have not been made in the petition (or answer claiming relief) then leave is required,[18] unless the parties are agreed on terms.

10-13   The Costs Rules

10-13.1   New costs rules for ancillary relief proceedings came into force on 3 April 2006.[19] A new costs rule (FPR r 2.71) is introduced, and FPR rr 2.69, 2.69B and 2.69D are omitted.

10-13.2   In ancillary relief applications made from 3 April 2006, the general rule is that 'the court will not make an order requiring one party to pay the costs of another party, but ... may make such an order at any stage of the proceedings where it considers it appropriate to do so because of the conduct of a party in relation to the proceedings (whether before or during them)'.[20]

10-13.3   The new rules include a list of factors which must be taken into account in deciding on any costs order. The factors can be summarised as: litigation conduct; open offers to settle; and the financial effect of any costs order.

---

[15]   FPR r 1.2(1).
[16]   Note the renumbering as from 5.12.2005.
[17]   FPR r 2.53(1).
[18]   FPR r 2.53(2).
[19]   The Family Proceedings (Amendment) Rules 2006 (SI 2006/352).
[20]   FPR r 2.71(4), as inserted by the FP(A)R 2006.

10-13.4   The new rules require the court to 'have particular regard to the extent to which each party has complied with the requirement to send documents with Form E'.[21]

10-13.5   'Calderbank' letters (ie marked 'without prejudice, save as to costs') will no longer be admissible at any stage, except for FDR purposes.[22] Only open offers to settle will be admissible in evidence.

10-13.6   This does not prevent parties using 'without prejudice' offers between themselves. Nor does it prevent without prejudice correspondence being adduced where it is said that a concluded agreement has been reached in that correspondence.

10-13.7   The new costs rules do not apply[23] to:

(1)   an application for ancillary relief made in a petition or answer issued before 3 April 2006;

(2)   an application in Form A or Form B issued before 3 April 2006;

(3)   an application in Form A or Form B issued after 3 April 2006 but heard at the same time as an application made before 3 April 2006.

10-13.8   In some cases it will therefore be important to know the date the petition (or answer) is issued. This is usually not the date at the end of the petition (or answer) – the filing date is often later.

10-13.9   Watch out for a petition which is filed before 3 April 2006, but an answer which is filed on or after that date. If the suit proceeds on the answer, and the petition is dismissed, then the new costs rules apply.

10-14   Ancillary Relief: The Application Form

10-14.1   All claims by the petitioner and virtually all claims by a respondent are proceeded with or made by filing Form A.[24]

10-14.2   Claims by other persons are also by Form A.[25]

10-14.3   A respondent's claim under s 10(2) MCA 1973 or s 48(2) CPA 2004 is the exception (consideration before decree absolute/CP final order of financial position in 2 year and 5 year separation petitions). This is made using Form B.[26]

---

[21]   FPR r 2.61D(2)(e), as substituted.
[22]   FPR r 2.71(6).
[23]   FP(A)R 2006 r 10.
[24]   FPR rr 2.53(2), (3), and 2.61A.
[25]   FPR r 2.54.
[26]   FPR rr 2.45(1) and 2.51B(1).

10-15 Titles: 'Applicant' and 'Respondent'; 'Husband' and 'Wife'

10-15.1 The ancillary relief rules and the prescribed forms refer to 'applicant' and 'respondent' (ie. applicant and respondent to the application). Unfortunately, this terminology can create considerable confusion when drawing orders.

10-15.2 This confusion is particularly acute in a number of circumstances:

- Where there are 2 concurrent applications. Who is the 'applicant'?

- Where the respondent to the petition is the applicant in the financial application, and the petitioner is then the respondent to the application. Who is the respondent?

- Where the respondent to a previous application is the applicant in a new application to vary. Who are the applicant and respondent when you vary the previous order?

10-15.3 To avoid confusion, some judges and practitioners have taken to referring to the parties as 'husband' and 'wife' in orders. But these descriptions cannot be used in civil partnership cases. The court should use a consistent practice in all types of suit.

10-15.4 The use of 'husband' and 'wife' is also contrary to the 2005 President's Direction relating to the title of causes.[27] (See the detail in *Marriage or Civil Partnership: Title of Parties, para 6-02 above*). This Direction was prompted by the Gender Recognition Act 2004, and is given emphasis by the introduction of the Civil Partnership Act 2004.

10-15.5 A solution is to revert to the longstanding (and probably better) practice of using the title of the parties as they appear in the main suit, ie. 'petitioner' and 'respondent'. Even with consolidated cross petitions, there will be a 'lead petition', which will define who the petitioner is, and who the respondent, for use in subsequent directions and financial orders.

10-16 Directions

10-16.1 The 'overriding objective' of the rules is 'enabling the court to deal with cases justly'.[28]

10-16.2 This includes 'allotting to it an appropriate share of the court's resources, while taking into account the need to allot resources to other cases'.[29] Do not however rely on this to underestimate hearing times. Practitioners will tend to do this in an attempt to obtain an earlier hearing date. It is counterproductive.

---

[27] President's Direction of 5 April 2005: The Gender Recognition Act 2004: Procedure – Title of the Cause: [2005] 2 FLR 122.
[28] FPR r 2.51D(1).
[29] FPR r 2.51D(2)(e).

10-16.3   The court must further the overriding objective by 'active case management' which includes the control of disclosure of documents and the fixing of timetables.[30]

10-16.4   There is now in use at the PRFD a pre-printed form 'Financial Claims Directions Menu'. A copy is printed in the Specimen Orders section of these notes *(see para 21-12 below)*. This contains suggested common form paragraphs and wordings for frequently used directions. Use of these forms promotes consistency and makes the job of the court clerk simpler.

10-16.5   Virtually all directions in financial ancillary relief (FAR) applications are given during the first appointment, adjourned first appointment, or Financial Dispute Resolution (FDR) hearings, with the parties present. Agreed directions (as paperwork) are now rare.

10-16.6   Under the rules, the first hearing is named the 'first appointment'. Some courts have adopted the practice of calling it the First Directions Appointment, for reasons which are unclear.[31] The Principal Registry uses the description prescribed in the rules.

10-16.7   When giving directions the court has the express objective[32] of 'saving expense' and 'dealing with the case in ways which are proportionate'. Whilst therefore the court may decide not to interfere too heavily in agreed directions, the court has to be satisfied they are justified, and is not obliged to approve them.

10-16.8   Even where directions are agreed, check that these are (i) within the court's jurisdiction, and (ii) capable of having practical effect.

10-16.9   In a suitable (unusual) case you may modify or dispense with some requirement of the rules, eg. direct that an affidavit stand as a Form E; or extend or abridge times.

10-16.10   Where an act is to be done (eg. a Form E or affidavit to be filed and served; or a report to be served or questionnaire answered) the modern practice is to give precise calendar dates for compliance.

10-16.11   If for any reason a particular date is not fixed, but instead a period is specified, then the direction must include the date from which time runs, eg. within 28 days from the date of this order, otherwise it is invalid.[33]

10-16.12   Leave of the court is required for any disclosure of documents[34] beyond that necessary to explain or clarify Form E. Disclosure usually dominates the First Appointment.

10-16.13   It is often convenient to give a common date for disclosure by both parties.

---

[30]   FPR r 2.51D(6).
[31]   Coyness about the abbreviation 'FA'? This not shared by the Principal Registry.
[32]   FPR r 2.51D(2).
[33]   See *Hitachi Sales (UK) v Mitsui Osk Lines* [1986] 2 Lloyds Rep 574, CA. CCR Ord 22 r.3 and RSC Ord 42 r.2.
[34]   FPR r 2.61B(6).

10-16.14 Record your decisions about disclosure by amending or writing on the questionnaires. Date and sign the copy which has your amendments marked on it.

10-16.15 If the amendments to the questionnaires are numerous or detailed it may be unnecessarily time consuming to recite them all expressly in an order.

10-16.16 **Do not direct that replies to questionnaires, or reports, be filed (they need only be served on the other party). Unnecessary filing of documents causes the staff extra work as well as increasing the size of court files.**

10-16.17 A short form direction may suffice in many cases:

> Order: Short Form: Replies to Questionnaires
>
> The Petitioner and Respondent must each provide to the other by [4.00pm on 31 January 2009] the information and copy documents requested in the respective questionnaires as amended by the court'.

10-16.18 However, this form of order is not suitable if a penal notice is to be attached. (See the section *'Penal Notices'- para 14 below*; and the alternative wording in *'Order Menu – Directions (Financial Ancillary Relief)' – para 21-12 below*.)

10-17   Fixing Hearings Including FDRs

10-17.1 The rules require the court to direct that hearings be fixed.[35] Wherever possible, fix the hearings with the parties and their advisers present. If for example the list office is unavailable, attempt to agree a hearing or trial 'window' and ask your clerk to obtain a date and insert it in the order before it is perfected and sent out.

10-17.2 Do not make orders which direct that a hearing be 'set down on the application to the list office by [counsel's clerks]' (or similar). Such directions have a poor record of efficient performance by practitioners.

10-17.3 Where counsel wish to check their chambers dairies for availability, fix the date in court and allow the parties to mention the case again later in the day if the date is inconvenient. On most occasions it is not necessary to change the date.

10-17.4 Only exceptionally should a case be adjourned generally.[36]

10-17.5 Be sceptical of claims that an FDR hearing will serve no purpose because compromise or settlement is unlikely. Experience shows that even some seemingly difficult cases do settle because of FDRs. But you may dispense with an FDR hearing if one is 'not appropriate'.[37] FDRs should usually be fixed between 8-12 weeks after the First Appointment.

---

[35] FPR rr 2.51B(6)(f), 2.61A(5), 2.61D(2)(d), 2.61E(8).
[36] FPR r 2.61D(2)(d)(iv).
[37] FPR r 2.61D(2)(c).

10-17.6   Do not fix a later final hearing as well as an FDR. Even if the final hearing must
           then take place some months after the FDR, this will still be significantly quicker
           overall (from issue of application to disposal) than under the old scheme.

10-17.7   It is now possible (but not routine) to fix FDRs and final hearings in ancillary
           relief before some circuit judges at the PRFD. The decision to do so is based on
           listing convenience. The PRFD has circuit judges who are identified as
           experienced in financial applications. Those circuit judges and the PRFD district
           judges exercise equal jurisdiction in ancillary relief matters.

10-17.8   If a financial ancillary case is transferred to the High Court, then fix the FDR
           before a High Court judge. Obtain a date from the Clerk of the Rules before the
           parties and their advisers leave court. Do not leave it to them to fix the date.

10-17.9   When you have fixed the date and time of the FDR, then include a direction that:

           Order: Attendance before FDR Appointment

           Both parties and their legal advisers (if any) must attend court on *{date
           and time – 1 hour before hearing}* for the purpose of negotiation.

10-18   Agreement Reached but Minutes to be Drafted

10-18.1   Frequently parties will reach agreement at or before a first appointment or FDR,
           but will require time to draw up the consent minute. Do not simply make no
           order. Do not adjourn the case without a date, to await the consent minute. This
           does not comply with the rule of 'fixing timetables or otherwise controlling the
           progress of the case'.[38]

10-18.2   Note the rule that 'the first appointment, or any subsequent appointment, must
           not be cancelled except with the court's permission and, if cancelled the court
           must immediately fix a new date'.[39]

10-18.3   A convenient solution is to use the mention date system. Fix a mention date (this
           will be at 10.30 am with a time estimate of 5 minutes only):

           Order: Mention Date awaiting Consent Minute

           The application(s) for ancillary relief is (are) listed for mention before DJ
           PRFD on *{date}* at 10.30am (time estimate 5 minutes).

           The mention date may be vacated if before then a consent minute has
           been approved by the court'.

10-18.4   This is a 'non attendance' hearing designed only to enable a district judge to
           consider the file briefly and, if necessary, direct a further mention date or other
           hearing.

---

[38]   FPR r 2.51D(6)(f).
[39]   FPR r 2.61A(5).

10-18.5 Do not fix this date too early. 6–8 weeks ahead is preferable. Do not use the mention date as a time when the consent minute itself will be considered. It is essentially a 'back-stop' date to check compliance. This allows the parties to agree and lodge a final draft, with sufficient time for a paperwork referral to a district judge to be completed. Shorter dates are often not complied with and simply create extra work for the staff handling further letters requesting more time.

10-19 Mention Dates

10-19.1 Mention dates are 5 minute (non attendance) slots put in the list at 10.30 am before other cases, on any date of your choosing. Your clerk must tell the list office of the date. No court time is actually allocated for a mention.

10-19.2 Please refer to the section: *Court Listing: Mention Dates (para 12 below)*.

10-19.3 **The mention date system must be <u>used only</u> as described in that section. Misuse of mention dates makes the system unworkable.**

10-20 FDR – Defended Petitions

10-20.1 Where the petition is defended you may list an FDR in respect of the financial claims. Sometimes settlement of the financial claims may promote agreement over the defended petition. **But in no circumstances should you fix a final hearing in the ancillary relief whilst the petition remains defended.**

10-21 FDR – Agreed Terms: No Binding Order

10-21.1 It is important to be clear about whether the court has made an order if it 'approves' agreed terms in a financial ancillary relief case.[40] Generally, it is poor practice to use the term. If it is <u>before</u> a decree/partnership order, the court can only order 'maintenance pending suit/outcome' – a final financial order cannot be made. If it is <u>after</u> a decree/partnership order, then 'approval' is ambiguous.

10-21.2 It frequently occurs that at court (during an FDR or other hearing) the parties arrive at heads of agreement, but require time to deal with the detail, including drafting the consent minute. Negotiations about some of the further detail may be crucial to the agreement. Some detail may not be significant.

10-21.3 If you indicate that the agreement is reasonable, both you and the parties should know whether or not you are intending to make an order. You should state this expressly. You should ask whether the parties want a final order that day, or simply an indication. The parties may be keen to have an order there and then, but this may not be possible or desirable for various reasons.

---

[40] See the difficulties in *Rose v Rose* [2002] EWCA Civ 208, 1 FLR 978.

10-21.4   The **basic principles** are:

(1)   the word 'approved' is ambiguous, and should not be used (or endorsed on the agreement) in these circumstances.

(2)   it is for the court (us):

•   to make clear to the parties what the court is doing;

•   to decide whether or not to make a substantive order;

•   to decide whether or not our remarks in an FDR are intended as an order or only a confidential indication.

10-21.5   If a final order is intended, there must be a decree/ partnership order <u>and</u> the terms of the agreement must be sufficiently certain and complete for the agreement to be made readily into a perfected order.

10-21.6   **If you accept the agreed terms in such a way that you are making a final order, then the draft perfected terms must be referred back to you (not someone else) for your final approval and signature.**

10-21.7   Whether the court makes a substantive order or not, the parties' heads of agreement will still be an *Edgar* agreement, if the parties agree that the terms are an 'open' agreement (ie not 'closed' or confidential).

10-21.8   For deputy district judges, it may be inconvenient for perfected terms to be referred back to you after your sitting period ends, and it may cause the staff more work. **As a deputy, it may be better either to sign the perfected terms before your sitting ends or, if that is not possible, to avoid making an order which requires later perfection.**

10-22   *FDR – Agreed Terms: Giving an Indication Only*

10-22.1   If you intend only an indication – then explain:

•   I am not making a final (substantive) order.

•   My indication is confidential.

•   The agreement seems reasonable (if appropriate).

•   If an agreed minute is lodged later, the court (probably a different district judge) will then consider whether to give its approval.

10-22.2   In any event you should specifically ask whether any agreed terms are 'open' or 'confidential' (closed).

10-22.3   If the agreed terms are 'open' (as will usually be the case), but you have given only a confidential indication, then it may be appropriate to list the matter for a mention date. This date should be sufficiently far ahead to allow a draft minute to be lodged by post and considered as paperwork before the mention date. **Do not make this date too early, this simply generates extra work. A date in 6–8 weeks is usual, as a 'back-stop' date to check compliance.** Do not use the mention date as a time when the consent minute itself is to be considered.

10-22.4   The suggested terms of **an order after an indication only** (but with an open agreement) would be:

> Order: A Mention after an Indication Only
>
> On the parties having agreed written heads of agreement dated *{date}*
>
> ORDER
> 1.   The application[s] for financial ancillary relief [is] [are] listed for mention before a DJ PRFD on *{date}* at 10.30 am (time estimate 5 minutes).
> 2.   The mention date may be vacated if before then a consent minute has been approved by the court.

10-23   *FDR – Agreed Terms: an Unperfected Binding Order*

10-23.1   If you intend to make a final order (subject to perfection), then:

Check:

- Whether there is a decree/partnership order.

Explain:

- I am making a binding order today in the terms of your agreement.

- But I am adjourning the application so that the detailed terms can be perfected into a final order.

- If you then disagree about those detailed final terms, the court will decide what those terms will be.

10-23.2   **If the heads of agreement are sufficiently complete** and the parties want a binding order immediately, but with perfected terms to be drafted later – then endorse the agreement with a note: 'O/ as agreed, in terms to be perfected. List before me on *{date}* as a mention'.

10-23.3   The suggested full terms of the (then) **unperfected order** are:

> Order: For an Unperfected Binding Order
>
> On the parties having made written heads of agreement dated *{date}*
>
> ORDER

1. (By consent) The heads of agreement dated *{date}* are made an order of the court in terms to be perfected by the court.
2. The parties are to draft the agreed proposed terms of the perfected final order [and lodge a written copy of those terms with the court by 4 pm on *{date}*].
3. The application[s] for financial ancillary relief [is] [are] listed for mention before DJ PRFD (reserved to D/DJ *{your own name}*) on *{date: 6-8 weeks ahead}* at 10.30 am (time estimate 5 minutes).
4. The mention date may be vacated if before then the perfected final order is made.

10-23.4   **The district judge's name and the date for the perfected final order must then be the same as that of the unperfected order**. This is because the final order is made when the heads of agreement are made an order of the court, even if those terms are unperfected at that time.

10-24   *Narrative Statements*

10-24.1   When fixing and giving directions for a final hearing you should usually direct that the parties serve and file concise narrative sworn statements (perhaps limited to particular issues) a few weeks before the hearing. Such statements are not necessary if the schedules of issues and Form Es are already adequate, though this is rarely the case.

10-24.2   For final hearings of 2 days or more in length, narrative statements are always needed. For shorter hearings they are still likely to be very useful.

10-24.3   These statements identify the facts and issues for the final hearing, set out the up to date position, give reasons for the orders sought and put the parties on notice of the case. Statements may also speed up the hearing because they can stand as the evidence in chief for each party.

10-24.4   The timing for service and filing of these statements is usually simultaneous, not sequential. Do not direct sequential exchange unless there are allegations (for example, conduct) which may require a process of charge and answer – such occasions will be rare.

10-24.5   It is usually not desirable for statements to be filed or served during an earlier phase of the application. For example, they should not be directed before the FDR. This creates extra expense, and rarely adds to the efficacy of an FDR appointment.

10-25   *Fixing the Final Hearing – Is there a Decree?*

10-25.1   There is nothing to prevent Form A being filed and directions being given before the decree nisi or of judicial separation (in marriage) or (in civil partnership) a conditional dissolution or separation order.

10-25.2 An FDR may also be listed before a decree or partnership order. Any agreement can be embodied in a consent minute and be made an order on pronouncement of the decree/partnership order (*see: 'Consent Orders and SP Petitions', para 10-29 below*).

10-25.3 But the final hearing must not be listed for hearing on a date before the decree nisi/conditional order is pronounced. The court has no jurisdiction to make final orders until the grant of a decree/civil partnership order.[41]

10-25.4 Normally if the decree/partnership order has not been pronounced, the final hearing date for financial claims should not be fixed (even for a date after pronouncement – there may be no decree/order for some reason). Unusually, on specific application, a date for the final FAR hearing may be fixed if the district judge's certificate has been signed and a date fixed for pronouncement.

10-25.5 Do not accept assurances or undertakings that the SP directions will be applied for. There are many times when this is not done. There may also be some other delay in the pronouncement of the decree/partnership order. This is true even when there is a completed acknowledgement of service on the court file.

10-25.6 This problem frequently occurs during an FDR when the parties realise that directions for trial have not been applied for in an undefended petition. Usually this is because they have been concentrating on the money claims. The parties then want a final hearing listed. A mention date may be a useful way of dealing with this problem (see below).

10-26 FDR – Using a Mention Date to Fix a Hearing

10-26.1 In an undefended petition, if after an FDR a final hearing is needed for the ancillary relief claims but there is no decree/partnership order granted or listed, then one economical solution is as follows:

(1) Give those directions which you can in the financial claims, but without fixing a final hearing.

(2) Include some provisional timetabling of the final evidence and trial bundles (in the form of, say, '[6 weeks] before the final hearing' etc).

(3) Use a mention date direction, such as:

Order: Mention Date to Fix a Final Hearing

The financial claims are listed for mention before DJ PRFD on *{date in, say, 6-8 weeks}* at 10.30 am (time estimate 5 minutes) for the purpose only of fixing a date for a final hearing.

---

[41] See ss 23(1), 24(1) and 24B MCA 1973 – all use the words 'On granting a decree ... or at any time thereafter ... the court may make [an order] ...'. Similar wording is used in civil partnerships: Sch 5 para 1 CPA 2004.

10-26.2 Once the final hearing is known, the only further final timetabling required may be to insert dates in the provisional timetable. This may be done on the mention. If any significant hearing is required to fix the timetable, then do not use the mention date system.

10-26.3 This 'mention system' ensures that a district judge will have to look at the file and be able to see whether the decree has been pronounced or listed. The court staff have no system or resources to monitor cases generally.

10-27 Consent Orders – General Matters

10-27.1 FPR r 2.61 provides a strict requirement for the standard short form information to be provided ('there shall be lodged') on applications for consent orders for financial relief. Check that this information, though brief, is apparently full and complete.

10-27.2 Watch for the filing of a Form A after a party has remarried or re-formed a civil partnership. A party who has remarried (or formed a new civil partnership) has no claims save those already made before such remarriage or re-formation.[42]

10-27.3 Where a party is acting in person and the other party is legally represented, some district judges ask the party in person to confirm in writing whether they have had the opportunity to seek legal advice about the agreement. This is not always asked for, but may be prompted by some unusual or apparently disadvantageous feature in the agreement.

10-28 Consent Orders – Dismissal of Claims

10-28.1 When claims are dismissed in consent orders, the practice in the PRFD is to require the filing of a Form A 'for dismissal purposes', unless the claims have been made in the petition or answer. A joint notice of application for an order in the agreed terms set out in the draft consent order may be sufficient.

10-28.2 See further points on the dismissal of claims under the section *'Common Drafting Errors' (para 10-32 below)*.

10-29 Consent Orders and SP Petitions

10-29.1 If the consent financial application accompanies an SP application, or comes up for consideration between the signing of the district judge's SP certificate and the pronouncement of decree, then refer to the earlier guidance (See: *para 6-28 above – 'The SP Certificate and Consent Orders for Ancillary Relief'*).

---

[42] Section 28(3) of the MCA 1973 and Sch 5 Part 10 para 48 CPA 2004.

10-30   *Pension Claims – Procedure and the Order*

10-30.1   An application for a pension order (whether sharing or attachment) must be served on the person responsible for the pension arrangement.[43]

10-30.2   No consent order for pension attachment may be made unless the person responsible for the pension arrangement has been served with notice of the application, a copy of the draft order, and some required details, and either no objection is made or any objection has been considered by the court.[44]

10-30.3   Look at the tick box on the statement of information to see if it confirms that the 'person responsible' has been served (and no objection received).[45]

10-30.4   The proper form of a pension order is:

Order: Pension Sharing/Attachment

There is to be provision by way of pension [sharing] [attachment] in accordance with the annex[es] to this order.[46]

10-30.5   There must be one annex for each pension arrangement, and the annexes must be in the prescribed form:[47]

(1)   Form P1 for pension sharing.

(2)   Form P2 for pension attachment.

10-30.6   A pension sharing order takes effect 21 days after the financial order or decree absolute/final partnership order (or determination of any appeal), whichever is later.

10-30.7   If pension attachment and the order is by consent, the annex in Form P2 requires the court to confirm (as the case may be) that either:

(1)   no objection has been made by the person responsible for the pension arrangement; or

(2)   an objection has been received and considered by the court.

10-31   *Deferring Enforcement of Legal Aid Statutory Charge*

10-31.1   The approved form[48] of the certificate under regulations 96 and 97 of the Civil Legal Aid (General) Regulations 1989 to defer the statutory charge is:

---

[43]   FPR r 2.70(6) – pension sharing. FPR r 2.70(7) – pension attachment.
[44]   FPR r 2.70(11) and (12).
[45]   FPR r 2.61(1)(dd).
[46]   FPR r 2.70(13).
[47]   FPR r 2.70(13).
[48]   Senior District Judge's Direction: 19 August 1991 – Family Division Directions p H4.

Order: Deferred Enforcement of Legal Aid Charge

It is certified for the purpose of the Civil Legal Aid (General) Regulations that:

[the lump sum {of £x} {payable under paragraph N of this order} has been ordered to be paid to enable the petitioner/respondent to purchase]

[the property {address} has been preserved/recovered for the petitioner/respondent for use as]

a home for himself/herself (or his/her dependants).

10-32   *Common Drafting Errors*

10-32.1   Do not make a 'no order' final order in financial ancillary relief since this is ambiguous.

10-32.2   The proper alternatives are:

   (1)   to make one of the permitted substantive orders, eg. for payment of money or transfer of property;

   (2)   to adjourn the application; or

   (3)   to dismiss it (with or without a direction as to making further claims – see sec 25A(3) MCA 1973 or Sch 5 para 23(4) CPA 2004).

10-32.3   Orders must be directed towards a party – ie. 'the respondent do transfer to the petitioner', not 'the property be transferred to the petitioner'. The only occasion this practice might not be followed is on a sale of a property when, for example, payments may be directed to be paid from the net proceeds to a party/person.

10-32.4   Periodical payments cannot be backdated before the date of the filing of the application (ie. the date of the petition or answer where claims are made therein, or the filing of Form A).[49] A variation may be backdated before the application to vary if fairness requires it,[50] though this is an unusual step. In any event, arrears accrued before the date of application can be remitted where a reduction is made.

10-32.5   A direction to bar further claims[51] applies only to claims under s 23(1)(a) or (b) MCA 1973 or Sch 5 para 2(1)(a) or (b) CPA 2004 [periodical payments and secured periodical payments]. Other claims cannot be barred with such a direction. But the remaining ancillary relief claims can be dismissed, after which no claim of the same type can be made again.

---

[49]   See s 28(1)(a) MCA 1973 or Sch 5 para 47(1) CPA 2004.
[50]   *S v S* [1987] 2 All ER 312; *Cornick v Cornick (No 2)* [1995] 2 FLR 490.
[51]   Under s 25A(3) MCA 1973 or Sch 5 para 23(4) CPA 2004.

10-32.6   The court cannot dismiss financial claims in other or future proceedings which have yet to be made. For example, it is common to find drafts which dismiss 'any claims under s 17 of the Married Women's Property Act 1882' or 'any claims arising under similar or replacing legislation'. The court has no power to dismiss any such claims, and the words should be struck through. A recital to similar effect as a preamble to the order may be acceptable, but should not extend to future legislation.

10-32.7   Do not dismiss periodical payments claims whilst taking an undertaking to pay continuing outgoings. This limits the relief the court can order in the event of non compliance, and the continuing obligation shows that the periodical payment claims should be retained.

10-32.8   Do not make dismissal of claims dependent on continuing obligations being performed. For example, a recital which says: 'upon the Respondent agreeing to pay the endowment policy premiums ...' followed by an order which dismisses the periodical payment claims. When does the dismissal take effect?

10-32.9   Draft terms sometimes provide for the dismissal of all remaining claims without making such dismissal dependent upon performance of the other parts of the order. Also sometimes agreed terms provide for the dismissal of Inheritance Act claims of a party in whose favour a continuing maintenance order is made. Such dismissals may not always be intentional and you may wish to query these provisions.

10-32.10 Avoid contradictory orders, eg. a lump sum order followed by a provision dismissing 'all claims'. The defect can be remedied by inserting, eg. 'all *remaining* claims' be dismissed.

10-32.11 Check that a date is provided for payment of a lump sum or transfer of property. 'Forthwith' is sufficient and means as soon as reasonably practicable. The better modern practice favours a specific period or date, since that reduces the room for later argument.

10-32.12 You cannot order undertakings or agreements – these can be recited as a preamble to the order itself.

10-32.13 There is no power to vary a lump sum or transfer of property order, except as to timing provided that time is 'not of the essence' in the order,[52] or except where a lump sum is payable by instalments.[53]

10-32.14 A second (later) lump sum or property adjustment order for a spouse can now be made on a variation application, but <u>only</u> if it is supplemental to the discharge or termination of a periodical payments order.[54]

10-32.15 It remains possible to make an S v. S type order dismissing periodical payments, eg. 'upon payment by the Respondent to the Petitioner of a lump sum of £x' or

---

[52]   *Masefield v. Alexander* [1995] 1 FLR 100, CA.
[53]   S 31(2)(d) MCA 1973.
[54]   S 31(7A) MCA 1973 or Sch 5 para 53 CPA 2004.

'upon the respondent transferring {property} to the petitioner'. Such a provision is merely the operative condition for dismissal.

10-33   Common Doubts

10-33.1   Why should a wife/partner on income support consent to the dismissal of her/his claims, without any corresponding benefit?

10-33.2   Why should one of the parties, after a long marriage or partnership, get no or only a small share of the available capital, without some counterbalancing benefit?

10-33.3   Will the division on a 'Mesher' order give the wife/partner enough capital to provide her/himself with a home? Consider the parties ages and likely circumstances on enforcement of the charge.

10-33.4   Why should capital be paid to children who apart from the divorce/dissolution would have received it only on the death of both parents/partners?

10-33.5   Are there indemnities in respect of the mortgage in the event that the mortgagees refuse to consent to the transfer of the mortgage?

10-33.6   If there is a trust of land, what provision is there about outgoings and repairs? Also, is there provision that only one spouse or partner should reside in the property? Otherwise, after decree absolute, there is no power in one joint owner to exclude another;[55] 'home rights'[56] do not continue without a court order, and relief by way of an occupation order under Part IV of the Family Law Act 1996 may be restricted.[57]

10-33.7   Are collateral endowment policies dealt with?

10-34   Refusing to Make a Consent Order.

10-34.1   You should refuse to accept undertakings which are contrary to public policy or whose effects would be void as an agreement, eg. an undertaking not to apply for a variation (void under s 34(1) MCA 1973 or Sch 5 para 68 CPA 2004); or an undertaking not to apply under the Child Support Act 1991 (void under s 9(4) CSA 1991).

10-34.2   You may find such terms also recited as agreements. They are still void under the same statutory provisions, and it is better not to include void provisions as a preamble to a court order. If however they are expressed as (or amended to) statements of intention then you may decide to permit them to remain in the preamble.

---

[55]   *Bull v Bull* [1953] P 224.

[56]   Previously 'matrimonial home rights' – see amendments to s 30 Family Law Act 1996 by Sch 9 CPA 2004.

[57]   But there are now other rights and reliefs under ss 12, 13 and 14 of the Trusts of Land and Appointment of Trustees Act 1996.

10-34.3 A judge is no rubber stamp, and cannot be compelled to make an order just because it is asked for by consent. Refusal does not prevent the parties carrying into effect their agreement, but they may not get the court's approval for their arrangements. Where both parties are legally represented, however, you should be slow to interfere with what the parties perceive to be in their best interests (and you may not know all the reasons behind the agreement).

11   Child Support Act 1991 (as amended)

11-01.1   Section 8 of the Child Support Act 1991 restricts the court in making, varying or reviving periodical payments orders in relation to a child, but does not prevent 'top up' orders, 'school fee' orders, or 'disability' orders. Also the court may make a periodical payments order which is in all material respects in the same terms as a maintenance agreement.[1] But the agreement must be in writing. The agreed terms or consent application is a maintenance agreement for these purposes.

11-01.2   A court order for child maintenance made on or after 3 March 2003 prevents a CSA assessment, but only for a year after the order was made.[2] Thereafter a CSA assessment can, in effect, replace the court order.

11-01.3   Further, there is nothing to prevent periodical payments for a spouse being made or increased to take into account the obligation to maintain children living with that person (s 25(2)(b) MCA 1973), where no assessment is under payment through the Child Support Agency (now part of the Child Maintenance and Enforcement Commission, since 1 November 2008).

---

[1]   Child Maintenance (Written Agreements) Order 1993 (SI 1993/620).
[2]   Child Support Act 1991 s 4(10)(aa), as amended.

12   Court Listing: Mention Dates

12-01.1   **Mention dates are 5 minute slots put in the list at 10.30 am before other cases, on any date of your choosing. It is a 'non attendance' appointment. No extra time is allocated in the court list. It is simply a means of bringing a file to the attention of a district judge to check (on paper) compliance with a previous order.**

12-01.2   The system of mention dates was introduced as a device to keep track of ancillary relief applications, without adjourning it generally (which should now be done only exceptionally). Its main use is where the parties have agreed terms, but need time to draft the final order and lodge it as paperwork for approval. It provides a 'back-stop' date to look at the file.

12-01.3   The mention date is not intended to be used to consider the consent minute itself. The consent minute itself should be dealt with by the usual system of paperwork referrals. Do not therefore fix the mention too early – 6–8 weeks ahead is preferable. This should allow time for a normal paperwork referral to be completed.

12-01.4   See also:

- *Ancillary Relief: Mention Dates (para 10-19 above)*

- *Ancillary Relief: Using a Mention Date to Fix a Hearing (para 10-26 above)*

- *Ancillary Relief: FDR – Agreement but Minutes to be Drafted (para 10-18 above)*

12-01.5   Please therefore use a mention date only in the following way:

(1)   they are non-attendance appointments

(2)   use only in ancillary relief applications

(3)   the date must not be treated as any kind of substantive hearing

(4)   do not expand the time

(5)   do not list at any other time

(6)   do not use multiple mentions on the same date

(7)   do not use for any other purpose.

12-01.6   **Do not use mention dates in any other way. Misuse makes the system unworkable. In particular, do not list 'mentions' for 10 or 15 minutes. This encourages parties to attend and creates over-listing problems for the district judge dealing with the work.**

12-01.7   If the parties want a brief hearing, the Short Summons List may be suitable.

12-01.8   The court listing at the PRFD is currently an 'appointment' system. The unit of listing is 30 minute slots. The only exception to this is the specialised Short Summons list, which is divided into 5 minute slots, with practitioners able to book up to 3 slots (15 minutes). The Short Summons list is used for miscellaneous, on notice, brief applications, such as a respondent's application for the grant of a decree absolute.

13   Financial Claims: Other than 'Ancillary Relief'

13-01   *The Children Act 1989: Schedule 1*

13-01.1   Applications for financial orders under Schedule 1 of the Children Act 1989 are **not** claims for financial **'ancillary relief'**.

13-01.2   The financial ancillary relief rules do not apply to those applications.

13-01.3   However, if the parties agree (as they usually do) disclosure can be ordered to be by questionnaire. The parties may also agree to make use of Form E, for convenience.

13-02   *Using FDR-Style Hearings by Agreement*

13-02.1   In financial applications made under Schedule 1 of the Children Act 1989, it is now common at the PRFD for the court to direct an FDR-style hearing, if the parties agree (but not otherwise). The jurisdictional validity of this is not without doubt. However, this (consensual) approach is justified by the poverty of the procedural code provided for Schedule 1 applications in the FPR.[1] The procedure applied by the rules is more or less limited to 2 provisions.[2]

13-02.2   In a non ancillary relief claim, if you direct (by consent) an **FDR-style hearing** then use the following **directions**:

> Order for FDR-Style Hearing
>
> The application is listed for hearing before a DJ PRFD on *{date}* at *{time}* (time estimate [1 hour]), which hearing is directed (by consent) to be treated as subject to the same rules as an FDR appointment.
>
> Both parties and their legal advisers (if any) must attend court on *{date and time – 1 hour before hearing}* for the purpose of negotiation.

13-03   *Transfer of Tenancies: Schedule 7 of the Family Law Act 1996*

13-03.1   A power that is sometimes useful, though frequently overlooked, is that in Schedule 7 of the Family Law Act 1996 to order the transfer between spouses or civil partners[3] of some tenancies.

13-03.2   The jurisdiction arises on or after the grant of a decree of divorce, nullity or judicial separation or a civil partnership order of dissolution, nullity or separation.

---

[1]   The Court of Appeal approved the use of a quasi-ancillary relief procedure: *Morgan v Hill* [2006] EWCA Civ 1602, 3 FCR 620.

[2]   See FPR r 4.4(6) – the application and Form C10A; and FPR r 4.9(1) – the acknowledgment.

[3]   Amended to include civil partners by s 82 and Sch 9 CPA 2004.

13-03.3   The tenancies included are:

(1)   a protected or statutory tenancy under the Rent Act 1977;

(2)   a statutory tenancy under the Rent (Agriculture) Act 1976;

(3)   a secure tenancy under s 79 of the Housing Act 1985;

(4)   an assured tenancy or assured agricultural occupancy under Part 1 of the Housing Act 1988;

(5)   an introductory tenancy under Chap 1 of Part V of the Housing Act 1996.

13-03.4   The orders may take effect only on or after the decree of judicial separation or civil partnership separation order, or on decree absolute or final order in the case of divorce, civil partnership dissolution or nullity.

13-03.5   Such applications are not 'ancillary relief'. The FPR makes no express provision for how an application is to be made. Therefore the RSC and CCR apply. At High Court level (unlikely) the application is by originating summons, and at County Court level (more likely) the application is by originating application.[4]

13-03.6   The difference between this power and that under section 24 MCA 1973 (and Part 2 CPA 2004) is that, under Schedule 7 of the FLA 1996, the order itself effects the transfer. By contrast under the 1973 Act and the 2004 Act the order directs the party to transfer. If then that party fails to execute the document of transfer, a further application must be made to the court, for example, to obtain the execution under section 39 of the Supreme Court Act 1981.

13-04   *Inheritance (Provision for Family and Dependants) Act 1975*

13-04.1   Claims under the I(PFD)A 1975 may be heard by heard by district judges of the Principal Registry, in our capacity as High Court district judges (ie. not as a 'divorce county court').[5] The Civil Procedure Rules 1998 apply to such claims. They may be heard in chambers.

13-04.2   The CPR do not include FDR type hearings. The CPR are a modern set of rules, which do not include such 'confidential' hearings. It is doubtful whether we should agree to hold such hearings in these types of claims, but practitioners often ask for them and district judges sometimes agree. If you do decide to hold an FDR type hearing in an Inheritance claim, this should be done only if the parties expressly agree, and an appropriate direction given. (See *Using FDR-Style Hearings by Agreement, para 13-02 above*).

---

4   RSC Ord 5 r 3 (High Court); Ord CCR Ord 3 r 4 (County Court).
5   CPR Part 2 r 2.4. Para 3.2 CPR Practice Direction Part 2B: Allocation of cases to levels of judiciary. Practice Direction – Family Division, President's Direction 22 April 1999.

13-05   *Trusts of Land and Appointment of Trustees Act 1996*

13-05.1   Claims under ToLATA 1996 may be heard by district judges of the Principal Registry, in our capacity as High Court district judges (ie. not as a 'divorce county court').[6] The Civil Procedure Rules 1998 apply to such claims. They may be heard in chambers.

13-05.2   There are jurisdictional doubts about holding FDR hearings in ToLATA claims, for the same reasons as apply to Inheritance claims (see previously), unless (perhaps) the ToLATA claim is being heard together with an application for ancillary relief. If you do decide to hold an FDR type hearing in a ToLATA claim, this should be done only if the parties expressly agree, and an appropriate direction given. (See *Using FDR-Style Hearings by Agreement, para 13-02 above*).

13-05.3   Where there is a ToLATA claim and a concurrent ancillary relief application, then direct (where appropriate) that they be 'heard together'. Do not direct that they be 'consolidated'. Consolidation means that the 2 claims become one. But the procedural and costs rules which apply to the 2 applications are different. If you 'consolidate' them, which rules apply?

13-06   *Failure to Maintain: Marriage and Civil Partnership*

13-06.1   An application may be made on the ground that a spouse or civil partner 'has failed to provide reasonable maintenance' for a spouse/partner or a child of the family. The jurisdiction is given by section 27 of the Matrimonial Causes Act 1973 (marriage) or Schedule 5 Part 9 of the Civil Partnership Act 2004 (civil partnership).

13-06.2   They are not applications for 'ancillary relief'.[7] They are begun by originating application. FPR r 3.1 applies to these applications. The ancillary relief procedure of Forms E, First Appointment and FDR does not apply to them.

13-07   *Financial Relief after Foreign Divorce/Dissolution*

13-07.1   These are not applications for 'ancillary relief'. They are applications for 'financial relief' made under Part III of the Matrimonial and Family Proceedings Act 1984 (marriages) or Schedule 7 of the Civil Partnership Act 2004 (civil partnership). FPR r 3.18 applies to them.

13-07.2   However, some of the ancillary relief rules apply to them,[8] but this does not include the procedure of Forms E, First Appointment and FDR (ie. not the 'new rules').

---

6   CPR Part 2 r 2.4 and the Practice Directions previously referred to.
7   FPR r 1.2(1).
8   See FPR r 3.18(3).

13-07.3   Such applications must be made by originating summons, and **substantive orders may be made only in the High Court by a judge,**[9] **not a district judge.** Leave to apply may only be given by a High Court judge. For these purposes, 'a judge' means a High Court Judge of the Division or someone sitting as a High Court judge under section 9 of the Supreme Court Act 1981.

13-07.4   The powers of a district judge are limited to giving directions.

13-07.5   Many applications for financial relief after a foreign divorce are now between people of ordinary means (not multi-millionaires). Assuming no other complication, these would not otherwise be heard before a High Court judge. Such cases should be directed to be heard by a suitable PRFD circuit judge, sitting as a 'section 9' High Court judge. The PRFD has some circuit judges who are identified as experienced in financial applications.

---

[9]   FPR r 3.18(8).

14   Penal Notices

14-01.1   A direction requiring performance of some act and to which it is intended to attach a penal notice should preferably be in the form:

> Order: Form Required to Attach Penal Notice
>
> The petitioner/respondent must [make, swear, file and serve his/her Form E] within [14] days of service of this order upon [him/her].

> **not**   'within [14] days from today'
> **nor**   'by [31 January 2009]'

14-01.2   Both the latter wordings may give rise to practical difficulties of enforcement, since the order must be served within the 14 days or before the specified date for it to become enforceable by committal.[1]

14-01.3   If the specified date in the order has expired, a fresh order must be obtained for enforcement. In a suitable case, one solution to these difficulties may be to use combined wording, eg.

> Order: Form Useable with or without Penal Notice
>
> The petitioner/respondent must [make, swear, file and serve his/her Form E] by [31 January 2009] or if not done by that date then within [14] days of service of this order upon [him/her], whichever is later.

14-01.4   The original order may then be used with or without a penal notice attached.

14-01.5   An enforcement warning notice[2] must now usually be attached to a contact order under s 8 of the Children Act 1989. For other section 8 orders, leave to attach a penal notice is required[3]. Apart from those 2 situations, no direction or leave is required to attach a penal notice to other orders. In the county court 'the proper officer <u>shall</u>, if the judgment or order is in the nature of an injunction' indorse the penal notice (there is no discretion to refuse).[4] In the High Court the indorsement is done by the party seeking enforcement (or his solicitor).[5]

14-01.6   Most orders for directions do not include a penal notice until there has been some non compliance. It is therefore usual for this to be specifically requested if required (there is no discretion to refuse once the order is made). To help the court staff, you should note this on the letter/summons by writing 'NB penal notice to be endorsed', but do not make it part of the order, unless leave has to be given.

---

[1]   CCR Ord 29 r 1(2).
[2]   Children Act 1989 s 11I, inserted by s 3 Children and Adoption Act 2006, w.e.f. 8.12.2008.
[3]   FPR r 4.21A.
[4]   CCR Ord 29 r 1(3).
[5]   RSC Ord 45 r 7(4).

15   Non-Molestation and Occupation Orders (Family Law Act 1996)

15-01   *Breach of Non-Molestation Order a Criminal Offence*

15-01.1   The breach of non-molestation orders made since 1 July 2007 is now a criminal offence (as well as a civil contempt).[1] The breach of an occupation order remains only a civil contempt. The new statutory regime brings important changes in practice.

15-01.2   A (civil) power of arrest is no longer attached to a new non-molestation order, but may still be attached to an occupation order.

15-01.3   The 2 types of order have 2 different regimes for enforcement: a non-molestation order by criminal arrest and prosecution (or civil contempt without the power of arrest); an occupation order by civil contempt only (but with a civil power of arrest). The 2 types of order may however be used in combination.

15-01.4   New non-molestation orders create judge-made criminal offences. Effective enforcement will depend on the police and Crown Prosecution Service being able to prove a clear breach. Strong guidance[2] from the experience with ASBOs (anti-social behaviour orders) includes the following:

(1)   the terms of the order must be precise and capable of being easily understood by the respondent;

(2)   the prohibition must be reasonable, proportionate, realistic and practical;

(3)   the prohibition must be in terms which make it easy to identify, prosecute and prove a breach.

15-01.5   Do not therefore, for example, make an order which prohibits the respondent from 'pestering' the applicant (which was used in the old wording). What does the criminal offence of 'pestering' consist of?

15-01.6   If you make an order forbidding the respondent from contacting the applicant except through solicitors, then insert the name, address and telephone number of the applicant's solicitors' firm in the order. This makes the permitted method of contact simpler.

15-02   *Exclusion Zones*

15-02.1   When directing exclusion zones, it is better practice to use named streets as the boundary, rather than the (less clear) 'not to go within 100 metres of [a property]'. If excluding someone from a named street, check that it is not (for example) a main road which the respondent may need to travel along.

---

[1]   Section 1 Domestic Violence, Crime and Victims Act 2004; Commencement Order SI 2007/1845.
[2]   See *R v Boness* [2005] EWCA Crim 2395 paras 19-24, [2005] All ER 153.

15-02.2　An exclusion zone may be included in a non-molestation order. As well as prohibiting stalking behaviour, it may pre-empt trouble by reducing the chance of a meeting. It is often thought that an exclusion zone can be made only as part of an occupation order. But this is incorrect.[3]

15-02.3　If possible, it is usually preferable to frame an exclusion order (either from an address or from a zone) as a non-molestation order rather than an occupation order. This provides a single mode of enforcement by criminal prosecution, rather than splitting enforcement between the criminal and civil courts for different parts of the breach. Where the respondent has no rights of occupation at the excluded address, this causes no difficulty.

15-02.4　If the respondent has rights of occupation at the address from which he or she is being excluded, then the 2 types of order should be used in combination. Such rights commonly arise with joint owners, joint tenants, or a spouse or civil partner with 'home rights'. The court will need to make an occupation order to suspend or modify those rights.

15-02.5　An occupation order is needed if the respondent is in actual occupation and is to be ordered to leave.

15-02.6　Suggested wordings are included in the Order Menu forms in the 'Specimen Orders' section – *see paras 21-13 and 21-14 below*.

---

[3]　See *Burris v Azadani* [1995] 1 WLR 1372, CA; [1996] 1 FLR 266.

16   Adoption: Editing of Reports

16-01.1   In contested adoption proceedings, it is now usual for the applicants (prospective adopters) and the respondent parents to be provided with suitably edited copies of the usual local authority report[1] and any children's guardian's report. The party producing the report should be primarily responsible for the editing, but a frequent safeguard is to provide that the local authority and the children's guardian agree the editing.

16-01.2   Some information in those reports should however not be disclosed. The identity of the applicants and the child(ren)'s placement should be kept private from the parents (if it is a confidential serial number case). Also, the applicant's referees should be able to express their views confidentially, without disclosure to the applicant.

16-01.3   This results in a rather cumbersome order, but my suggested draft is as follows:

> Order: Adoption – Disclosure of Edited Reports
> 1.   The Local Authority shall by *{date}* serve an edited copy of its rule 29 report on the Applicants *{prospective adopters}* and the Respondent mother and father the editing to be agreed with the Children's Guardian.
> 2.   The Children's Guardian shall by *{date}* serve an edited copy of his/her report on the Applicants *{prospective adopters}* and the Respondent mother and father, the editing to be agreed with the Local Authority.
> 3.   The edited copies of the reports of the Local Authority and Children's Guardian served on the Applicants shall exclude any sections about references or referees, except for the names and addresses of the referees.
> 4.   The edited copies of the reports of the Local Authority and Children's Guardian served on the Respondent mother and father shall exclude: (a) any information which may identify the current placement of the child(ren) who is/are the subject(s) of the proceedings; (b) any information which may identify the Applicants; and (c) any sections about references or referees.

---

[1]   Commonly called a Rule 29 report: r 29 Family Procedure (Adoption) Rules 2005 (SI 2005/2795).

17   Production of Prisoners to Court

17-01.1   A district judge cannot order that a prisoner be produced to court. This may only be ordered by a judge.[1] A High Court judge may order a prisoner to be brought to court to give evidence.[2] A circuit judge also may order a prisoner to be brought before the court as a witness,[3] but not if his detention is under any civil process (eg. civil contempt).

17-01.2   In the case of a person who is 'remanded in custody', 'serving a sentence of imprisonment' or 'detained in a prison' in any part of the United Kingdom the Secretary of State (Home Office) may direct that that person be taken to any place in the United Kingdom if the Secretary of State is satisfied that the attendance of that person 'is desirable in the interests of justice'.[4]

17-01.3   This latter power is that usually used to request that a prisoner who is a party to proceedings attends court. The solicitor of a party should make the request directly to the prison governor[5] in the first instance. No court order is necessary. If confirmation is needed that the attendance is desirable for the hearing (or perhaps if a litigant in person needs guidance) the court may make a request in the form of an order. Such a request can be made by a district judge, but is not binding on the Prison Governor (Home Office). The place, date and time of attendance and hearing time estimate should all be given.

17-01.4   A suggested draft order of request is as follows:

Order: Request for Production of Prisoner (as a Party)

On hearing the oral request by [counsel] [solicitor] for {name}
On reading the letter of request dated {date} from the solicitors representing {name}

ORDER
1.   The Governor of *{name}* Prison is requested to produce *{name}* (who is a party to the proceedings) at court at the Principal Registry of the Family Division, First Avenue House, 42-49 High Holborn, London, WC1V 6NP for the purpose of a hearing on *{date}* at *{time}* (time estimate *{time}*).
2.   The court confirms that the personal attendance of *{name}* at the hearing is desirable in the interests of justice, if he/she wishes to attend.
3.   This order may be disclosed to the relevant Prison Governor.

---

[1]   See generally *Halsbury's Laws* 4th edn Vol 36(2) para 609; *Rayden* 18th edn Vol 1(1) para 17.73.
[2]   CPR Sch 1 RSC Ord 54 r 9(2).
[3]   Section 57 County Courts Act 1984.
[4]   Crime (Sentences) Act 1997 s 41 and Sch 1 para 3(*2). Halsbury's Statutes* 4th edn Vol 34 (2004 re-issue) p 1029. Note that s 29 Criminal Justice Act 1961 (which is still referred to in *Rayden* and *the White Book*) was repealed and replaced by C(S)A 1997 on 1.10.1997.
[5]   *White Book* 2008 Vol 1 sc54.9.

18   Disclosure of Addresses and Information from Non-Parties

18-01   Disclosure of Information: The Statutory Powers

18-01.1   The principal statutory provisions about disclosure of information (including addresses) from non-parties are:

(1)   Those which **do not bind the Crown**, namely:

- s 33 Family Law Act 1986

- s 24A Child Abduction and Custody Act 1985

(2)   Those which **do bind the Crown**, namely:

- s 34 Supreme Court Act 1981 (as amended)

- s 53 County Courts Act 1984 (as amended)

18-02   Disclosure of Information: s 33 Family Law Act 1986

18-02.1   The power to make disclosure orders under s 33 Family Law Act 1986[1] arises:

'where in proceedings for or relating to a Part 1 order in respect of a child there is not available to the court adequate information as to where the child is, the court may order any person who it has reason to believe may have relevant information to disclose it to the court.'

18-02.2   A 'Part 1 order' means:[2]

(1)   a section 8 order [under Children Act 1989] – other than an order varying or discharging such an order;

(2)   a special guardianship order [under s 14A Children Act 1989];

(3)   an order for contact under s 26 Adoption and Children Act 2002 – other than an order varying or discharging such an order;

(4)   an order made in the exercise of the inherent jurisdiction of the High Court with respect to children – so far as it gives care of a child to any person or provides for contact with, or the education of, a child but excluding an order varying or revoking such an order.

---

[1]   The wording in s 24A Child Abduction and Custody Act 1985 is identical, except that the proceedings must relate to that Act.

[2]   See s 1(1)(a) and (d) Family Law Act 1986, as amended by the Adoption and Children Act 2002.

18-02.3 Note that the power is to discover the whereabouts of the <u>child</u> and disclose the information to the <u>court</u>. Section 33 FLA 1986[3] gives <u>no jurisdiction to make disclosure orders</u> in respect of:

(1) - tracing adults (except as a way to find a relevant child); or

(2) - care proceedings (under s 31 CA 1989); or

(3) - adoption proceedings generally (except for contact under s 26 ACA 2002).

18-02.4 Neither s 33 FLA 1986 nor s 24A CACA 1985 binds the Crown. This was the reason for the Registrar's Direction 1989 on Disclosure of Addresses,[4] which was drawn up to achieve, by agreement, cooperation by relevant government departments, in the public interest of the proper administration of justice. **This cooperation allows information to be requested, but does not permit the court to make a mandatory order.**

18-03 *Disclosure of Information: s 34 Supreme Court Act 1981 and s 53 County Courts Act 1984*

18-03.1 Section 34(2) Supreme Court Act 1981 and section 53(2) County Courts Act 1984 are in identical terms and provide:

> '... the [High/County Court] shall, in such circumstances as may be specified in the rules, have power to order a person who is not a party to the proceedings and who appears to the court to be likely to have in his possession, custody or power any documents which are relevant to an issue arising out of the said claim ... to produce ... those documents ... to the applicant or, on such conditions as may be specified in the order –
>
> (i)   to the applicant's legal advisers; or
> (ii) to the applicant's legal advisers and any medical or other professional adviser of the applicant;
> (iii) if the applicant has no legal adviser, to any medical or other professional adviser of the applicant.'

18-03.2 These sections bind the Crown, but the court is not to make such an order if it considers that 'compliance with the order, if made, would be likely to be injurious to the public interest'.[5]

18-03.3 Originally these provisions were limited to claims for personal injuries or death. That limitation was removed in 1999, at the same time as the introduction of the Civil Procedure Rules. The provisions now apply to any proceedings in respect of

---

[3] The same limitation applies to s 24A Child Custody and Abduction Act 1985.

[4] Registrar's Direction 13 February 1989 – Family Division Directions pp A13-16. Set out in full in *Rayden & Jackson on Divorce and Family Matters*, 18th edn, Vol 1(2) para 55.120. See the detailed treatment in these notes at para 18-06 Disclosure of Information: Government Departments – The Registrar's Direction 1989.

[5] Section 35 Supreme Court Act 1981 and s 54 County Courts Act 1984. See the discussion in *the White Book* 2008 para 31.3.33. The principles are summarised *in R v Bromell, Re Coventry Evening Newspapers Ltd* [1993] QB 278.

which relevant rules are made. The Civil Procedure Rules 1998 and the Family Procedure (Adoption) Rules 2005 both contain new disclosure rules made under the amended primary legislation.[6]

18-03.4   Unfortunately, there are difficulties applying these amended sections to the Family Proceedings Rules 1991. The FPR and the Adoption Rules 1984 still incorporate the old unchanged pre-1999 RSC and CCR,[7] which limit the applications to claims for personal injuries.[8] It may be arguable that the RSC and CCR should now be 'read down' under the Human Rights Act 1998 to exclude the references to personal injuries claims. But the difficulties make the application of these sections to family proceedings uncertain (except to new adoption proceedings under the 2002 Act).

18-04   Disclosure of Information: Adoption and Children Act 2002

18-04.1   Rule 79 of the Family Procedure (Adoption) Rules 2005 contains a new rule for disclosure of documents in adoption applications made under the Adoption and Children Act 2002. This rule derives from s 34 SCA 1981 and s 53 CCA 1984. The jurisdiction is materially different to that under s 33 FLA 1986. In particular, in the 2005 Adoption Rules the power relates to 'documents' (though an electronic record may be a document) and disclosure is to the applicant or his legal, professional and medical advisers (not to the court).

18-04.2   Also, for service of new adoption applications under the 2002 Act, Part 6 and section 1 of the 2005 Adoption Rules is supplemented by a Practice Direction, which includes a section on 'Service on members of HM Forces'. This provides:[9]

> 'where a person to be served is known to be serving or to have recently served as a member of HM Forces the applicant's legal representative may obtain the address for service of proceedings under the Adoption and Children Act 2002 from the appropriate officer of the Ministry of Defence as specified in the table [in the practice direction].'

18-04.3   Note the limits in this Practice Direction. It permits a request, not a mandatory order. It does not apply to adoption proceedings under the Adoption Act 1976. Nor does it apply to other government departments.

18-05   Disclosure of Information: Government Departments – Current Guidance

18-05.1   As seen in the previous section, there are significant limits on the extent of any jurisdiction in family proceedings to <u>order</u> government departments to give disclosure of addresses of adults.

---

[6]   CPR 1998 r 31.17 and FP(A)R 2005 r 79.
[7]   FPR 1991 r 1.3(1) and AR 1984 r 3(2).
[8]   See RSC Ord 24 r 7A(2), applied to the County Court by CCR Ord 13 r 7(2A).
[9]   Family Procedure (Adoption) Rules 2005: para 4.1 Practice Direction Part 6 – Service, December 2005.

18-05.2   In so far as the court may <u>request</u> information (particularly addresses) from government departments, such requests should be made only in the limited circumstances covered by a relevant Practice Direction, Guidance or Protocol.

18-05.3   Orders and requests for disclosure of information and addresses by government departments are not routine, and you should check the court's jurisdiction before making them.

18-05.4   *Table 5: Government Departments – Addresses and Requirements (para 18-09 below)* gives a summarised guide to the common circumstances and methods in which disclosure may be sought, together with current relevant contact details.

18-05.5   There are specimen forms of order in the later sections of these notes.

18-05.6   The Practice Directions, Guidance and Protocols currently in force include:

- **Disclosure of Addresses** (by Government Departments) – The Registrar's Direction 13 February 1989, amended 1995.

- **Communicating with the Home Office** regarding immigration matters in family proceedings – President's Protocol, December 2002, revised January 2006.

- **Communicating with the Passport Service** in family proceedings – President's Protocol, August 2003.

- **Disclosure Orders against [HM Revenue & Customs]** – [formerly the 'Inland Revenue'] – Guidance from the President's Office, November 2003.

- **Service on members of HM Forces** – Adoption Practice Direction on Service, December 2005. Supplements Part 6, Section 1 of the Family Procedure (Adoption) Rules 2005 made under the Adoption and Children Act 2002.

18-06   *Disclosure of Information: Government Departments – The Registrar's Direction 1989*

18-06.1   The Registrar's Direction (Disclosure of Addresses) 1989[10] is still in force, but was last amended formally in 1995. It sets out the circumstances in which the court is able to <u>request</u> disclosure of addresses by government departments. It gives the details of the departments and their contact addresses which (then) may have been able to help (in order of likelihood). The Direction is set out in full in *Rayden & Jackson on Divorce and Family Matters*, 18th Edn, Vol 1(2) para 55.120.

18-06.2   The 1989 Direction provides that the court may request disclosure of addresses by government departments for the purpose of:

---

[10]   *Rayden & Jackson on Divorce and Family Matters*, 18th edn, Vol 1(2) para 55.120. See also [1988] 1 WLR 648. See Family Division Directions pp A13-16.

(1)   tracing the address of person in proceedings against whom another person is seeking to obtain or enforce an order for financial provision either for himself or herself or for the children of the former marriage; or

(2)   tracing the whereabouts of a child, or the person with whom the child is said to be, in proceedings under the Child Abduction Act 1985 or in which a 'Part 1 order' [ie. as defined in Part 1 of the Family Law Act 1986] is being sought or enforced.

18-06.3   The 1989 Direction also provides that in financial provision applications the court should certify either:

(1)   that a financial provision order is in existence, but cannot be enforced because the person against whom the order has been made cannot be traced; or

(2)   that the applicant has filed or issued a notice, petition or originating summons containing an application for financial provision which cannot be served because the respondent cannot be traced.

18-06.4   Note the limited circumstances in which such requests could be made, in particular that petitions must contain a prayer for financial relief, and in children matters the purpose is to trace the child, but only in 'Part 1' proceedings.

18-06.5   Since 1989 the names, responsibilities and contact details of some departments in the Direction have changed, as well as the statutory framework within which government departments hold their data.[11] The Direction must now be read subject to the more recent guidance, protocols and practice directions *(see para 18-05 above)*, as well as changes in some of the contact details and departmental responsibilities.

18-06.6   Importantly, the Department for Work and Pensions (formerly the Department of Social Security) no longer holds national insurance and child benefit records. These are now held by HM Revenue and Customs, which has strict statutory confidentiality obligations.[12] A search of the HMRC records requires a High Court order under its inherent jurisdiction.

18-06.7   The DWP cannot therefore normally be used to search for the whereabouts of a child. It still holds records for people on benefits such as Income Support, Incapacity Benefit, Disability Living Allowance and Attendance Allowance. Those will be of more limited use than the records held by the HMRC.

18-06.8   The DWP may still be used under the 1989 Direction to search for a person, provided it is for the purpose, either of seeking, obtaining or enforcing a financial order, or for tracing a person who may have a relevant child with them.

18-06.9   But since the DWP does not hold national insurance records, it will usually not be effective to find an address for the purpose of service of a financial application

---

[11]   See the Data Protection Acts 1984 and 1988.
[12]   Eg under the Taxes Management Acts.

(or a petition containing a financial claim). Also, for a search to trace a person with a relevant child, a HMRC search of the child benefit records will be more effective.

18-06.10 Note also that the addresses previously held by the Office for National Statistics (Traceline) and the NHS Central Register (NHSCR) have now (since 1st April 2008) been transferred to the Information Centre for Health and Social Care.

18-06.11 The 1989 Direction specifies that 'requests for such information will be made officially by the district judge'. For this reason, most departments now require a request for disclosure to be in the form of an order (an 'order of request'). An 'order of request' has the advantage that, whilst there is no mandatory requirement to reply, it shows that the request has the court's approval. Such requests are usually effective. (*See the 'Index to Specimen General Orders and Forms': para 20-01 below*).

18-06.12 However, an 'order of request' may be ambiguous and it should be used only in the circumstances covered by the Registrar's Direction 1989, a President's Protocol or a Practice Direction.

18-06.13 If a mandatory order is required, then the court must be satisfied as to the jurisdiction under which any order is being made. This jurisdiction is not straightforward.

18-07 Disclosure Orders against Other Third Parties

18-07.1 Because it is ambiguous in its meaning, an 'order of request' should not be used generally if addressed to non-parties who are not government departments.

18-08 Addresses for Contacting Government Departments

18-08.1 There follow 2 Tables with addresses for contacting Government Departments.

18-08.2 *Table 5: Government Departments – Addresses and Requirements (para 18-09 below)* gives a current list of contact details for government departments which may be able to help with enquiries. *Table 5* also gives a summarised guidance about the purpose, jurisdiction and methods of communicating with those departments.

18-08.3 Note that the addresses previously held by the Office for National Statistics (Traceline) and the NHS Central Register (NHSCR) have now (since 1 April 2008) been transferred to the Information Centre for Health and Social Care.

18-08.4 Samples of the orders suggested in *Table 5* are set out in the section *Specimen Orders and Forms of Request for Information (see para 21 below)*.

18-08.5   The key to abbreviations in *Table 5: Government Departments – Addresses and Requirements.*

ACA	– Adoption and Children Act 2002
CACA	– Child Abduction and Custody Act 1985
CCA	– County Courts Act 1984
FLA	– Family Law Act 1986
FP(A)R 2005	– Family Procedure (Adoption) Rules 2005
HMRC	– HM Revenue & Customs
HO	– Home Office
SCA	– Supreme Court Act 1981
UKPS	– UK Passport Service

18-08.6   *Table 6: Contact Addresses: HM Forces (para 18-10 below)* gives a list of addresses to contact service personnel in HM Forces.

18-09 **Table 5: Government Departments – Addresses and Requirements**

Department and Contact Address	Purpose, Jurisdiction and Method of Contact
HM Revenue & Customs Customer Relations Unit Child Benefit Office PO Box 1 Newcastle upon Tyne NE98 1AA	Whereabouts of child • Inherent jurisdiction • President's Guidance HMRC • High Court only • Order • Use INHERENT order • Disclose to court
HM Revenue & Customs National Insurance Contributions Office Special Section A BP 1002 Benton Park View Newcastle upon Tyne NE98 1ZZ	Whereabouts of adult • Inherent jurisdiction • President's Guidance HMRC • High Court only • Order • Use INHERENT order • Disclose to court
Home Office Immigration and Nationality Directorate Contact – send request in an order to: Family Division Lawyer President's Chambers Royal Courts of Justice Strand, London, WC2A 2LL T: 020 7947 7197 F: 020 7947 7274 also use for: UK Passport Service UK Visas These are all part of the Home Office. The Home Office style order and Form Ex 660 is therefore also used for enquiries of those agencies	Information (usually about immigration status) • President's Protocol Home Office • High Court or County Court • Request in an order • Use HOME OFFICE order & Form EX660 • Need following details (if known) of the child and both mother and father: – full name including middle names – date of birth – country of origin – date of arrival in UK – all known Home Office reference numbers • If used for UK Passport Service or UK Visas, the required details need to be adapted • Disclose to court (or as directed)

Department and Contact Address	Purpose, Jurisdiction and Method of Contact

Department for Work and Pensions
Data Protection Officer
Central London District Office
PO Box 10
Glasgow
G4 0HH
 	
NOTE:
DWP records are of very limited value for tracing addresses.
Child benefit and national insurance records are now held by HM Revenue & Customs.
HMRC requires a High Court inherent jurisdiction order under President's Guidance 2003 *(see earlier in Table 5, and in the text at para 18.05 above)*.
	Whereabouts of adult (with child). Whereabouts of person for the purpose of obtaining or enforcing financial provision order.
	• Registrar's Direction 1989
	• High Court or County Court
	• Request in an order
	• Use GENERAL order
	• Undertaking that information will be used only for purpose above
	• Certify: financial provision order exists but cannot be enforced; or application issued but cannot be served
	• Need following details (if known) for the person sought:
	  – full name
	  – date of birth
	  – last known address
	  – other relevant information
	• Disclose to court, solicitor or applicant

Health and Social Care Information Centre Smedley Hydro Trafalgar Road Birkdale Southport PR8 2HH (replaces Office for National Statistics & NHS Central Register)	Whereabouts of adult (with child). Whereabouts of person for the purpose of obtaining or enforcing financial provision order. • (As for Department for Work and Pensions)
Child Support Agency Ashdown House Sedlescombe Road North St Leonards East Sussex TN37 7NL	Whereabouts of child. Whereabouts of adult (with child). Whereabouts of person for the purpose of obtaining or enforcing financial provision order. • (As for Department for Work and Pensions)

Department and Contact Address	Purpose, Jurisdiction and Method of Contact

Ministry of Defence
 	
Contact addresses – see the list in Part 6 Practice Direction which supplements the Family Procedure (Adoption) Rules 2005
The list is reproduced below in Table 6 'Contact Addresses – HM Forces'
The addresses in the Registrar's Direction 1989, as amended in 1995, may now be out of date.
	Whereabouts of child.
	Whereabouts of adult (with child).
	Whereabouts of person for the purpose of obtaining or enforcing financial provision order.
	(Where the person sought is serving or recently served in HM Forces, for the purpose only of service of proceedings)
	
	• Registrar's Direction 1989
	• High Court or County Court
	• Letter from solicitor
	• Request in an order (for litigant in person)
	• Use GENERAL order
	• Undertaking that information will be used only for purpose above
	• Need following details (if known) of the person sought:
	  – full name
	  – date of birth
	  – service number, rank or rating
	  – unit (or similar) in which served
	  – date of start of service
	  – date of discharge
	  – last known address
	  – other relevant information
	• Disclose to solicitor and court
	• Not disclosed to applicant or any other person, except in the normal course of proceedings

Department and Contact Address	Purpose, Jurisdiction and Method of Contact
Ministry of Defence Contact – see the list of addresses in the Part 6 Practice Direction which supplements Family Procedure (Adoption) Rules 2005 The list is reproduced below in Table 6 'Contact Addresses – HM Forces'	Whereabouts of adult Adoption and Children Act 2002 only: (Where the person sought is serving or recently served in HM Forces, for the purpose only of issuing and service of proceedings) <ul><li>FP(A)R 2005: Part 6 Practice Direction</li><li>High Court or County Court</li><li>Letter from legal representative</li><li>(Probably) Request in an order (for litigant in person)</li><li>Use GENERAL order</li><li>Undertaking that information will be used only for purpose above</li><li>Need following details (if known) of the person sought: – full name – service number, rank or rating – unit (or similar) in which served – other relevant information</li><li>Disclose to legal representative and court</li><li>Not disclosed to applicant or any other person, except in the normal course of proceedings</li></ul>

Department and Contact Address	Purpose, Jurisdiction and Method of Contact
All Departments (Individual department details as set out previously)	Relevant documents Adoption and Children Act 2002 only: <ul><li>s 34 SCA 1981 & s 53 CCA 1984</li><li>r 79 FP(A)R 2005</li><li>High Court or County Court</li><li>Order</li><li>Use ADOPTION order</li><li>Application – Part 9 FP(A)R 2005</li><li>Evidence needed</li><li>Include right to apply to set aside or vary</li><li>Disclose to applicant or advisers</li></ul>

18-10   *Table 6: Contact Addresses: HM Forces*

18-10.1   The information in *Table 6* is reproduced from the Part 6 Practice Direction which supplements the Family Procedure (Adoption) Rules 2005, and was up to date at December 2005 (and was not varied in October 2007 by the amended rules).

HM Forces Contact Addresses	
Royal Navy Officers	The Naval Secretary Room 161 Victory Building HM Naval Base Portsmouth Hants PO1 3LS
RN Ratings	Commodore Naval Drafting Centurion Building Grange Road Gosport Hants PO13 9XA
RM Medical and Dental Officers	The Medical Director General (Naval) Room 114 Victory Building HM Naval Base Portsmouth Hants PO1 3LS
Officers of Queen Alexandra's Royal Naval Nursing Service	The Matron-in-Chief QARNNS Room 139 Victory Building HM Naval Base Portsmouth Hants PO1 3LS
Naval Chaplains	Director General Naval Chaplaincy Service Room 201 Victory Building HM Naval Base Portsmouth Hants PO1 3LS

HM Forces Contact Addresses	
Royal Marine Officers and Ranks	Royal Marines Personnel Section West Battery Whale Island Portsmouth Hants PO2 8DX
RM Ranks HQRM	Royal Marines (DRORM) West Battery Whale Island Portsmouth PO2 8DX
Army Officers and other ranks	Army Personnel Centre Secretariat, Public Enquiries RM CD424 Kentigern House 65 Brown Street Glasgow G2 8EH
Royal Air Force Officers and other Ranks	Personnel Management Agency (RAF) Building 248 RAF Innsworth Gloucester GL3 1EZ

18-10.2   The next section is *19. Principal Registry Common Form Orders* on the following pages.

19   Principal Registry Common Form Orders

19-01   How to Use the Specimen General Orders and Forms

19-01.1   Attached to these notes are a number of specimen orders and requests for information. The form of each of these specimens is either expressly provided for by the President's Guidance or is the preferred version for use in the Principal Registry of the Family Division.

19-01.2   These are the specimen orders and forms at *paragraphs 21-01 to 21-11 below*. These are forms for general use, but the text of the specimens is tailored for the Principal Registry. Minor changes are needed if used in other courts.

19-02   How to Use the Orders and Forms for Government Departments

19-02.1   If you require a search to be undertaken of the government department registers, ask the parties or their legal representatives to complete the relevant form of request for information, give those details to your clerk and make the appropriate order. Your clerk will forward the papers, either to the President's office or to a court manager (at the Principal Registry, this is currently Ruth Ewen, the deputy court manager).

19-03   Principal Registry Common Form Orders

19-03.1   For a number of years the Principal Registry has used Menu Forms which include common form orders in plain English. These forms (mainly for directions and the more formulaic orders) prompt the memory when making an order. Use of the agreed wording improves consistency and helps staff to draw up orders in a familiar style.

19-03.2   Copies are included in the 'Specimen Orders' section (*see paras 21-12 to 21-18 below*). The areas covered are:

(1)   ancillary relief directions (including valuations and experts)

(2)   non-molestation orders

(3)   occupation orders

(4)   prohibited steps and directions (private law Children Act)

(5)   Local Authority investigations (s 37 Children Act)

(6)   case management directions (public law Children Act)

(7)   instruction of experts (public law Children Act)

19-03.3   The menu forms for the public law Children Act are not substitutes for the Public Law Outline Draft Case Management Template, they are only my suggested wording for common paragraphs used to populate the template, which is then submitted to the court as directed in the PLO. The order of paragraphs follows the headings in the PLO draft template.

19-03.4   **Do not make orders for the routine filing of general documentary disclosure. This causes much unnecessary work for the staff, and makes files very bulky.**

20   Specimen Orders and Forms – Index

20-01   Index to Specimen General Orders and Forms

20-02   Index to Principal Registry Common Form Orders

21   Specimen Orders and Forms of Request for Information

21-01   *Order for Disclosure – Inherent Jurisdiction*

IN THE HIGH COURT OF JUSTICE
Principal Registry of the Family Division

Case Number:

The full name(s) of the child(ren):   Boy/Girl: Date(s) of Birth:

In the Matter of the Inherent Jurisdiction of the High Court

UPON HEARING [counsel] [solicitor] for ...., **the**

Applicant in this matter, [at a hearing without notice] [and] [counsel][solicitor] for ....

.... , **the [First] Respondent] [and   ]**

AND UPON the matter being transferred to the High Court for the purposes of this Application only.

THE COURT ORDERS THAT:

1.   HM Revenue & Customs, by its officers, servants or agents shall disclose, in writing, as soon as practicable to Ruth Ewen, Principal Registry of the Family Division, First Avenue House, 42-49 High Holborn, London WC1V 6NP all information in its knowledge or control of the whereabouts of [*name(s) and date(s) of birth of person(s) sought*]

2.   HM Revenue & Customs, by its officers, servants or agents shall not disclose the content of this order or any action they take pursuant to it, to   [*name(s) of person(s) sought*]

3.   There be liberty to HM Revenue & Customs to apply to vary or discharge this order upon 24 hours notice.

4.   Any information received by the court under this order *{ delete as appropriate }*
[will be confidential to the court and may not be disclosed to the parties without permission of the court]
[may be disclosed to the parties].

5.   This order is made on condition that any information received will be used only for the purpose of service of the proceedings

Ordered by
[Mr][Mrs] Justice
[His][Her]Honour Judge [   ] sitting as a Judge of the High Court
[Mr][Mrs][Ms] [   ] sitting as a Deputy High Court Judge
District Judge [   ] of the Principal Registry of the Family Division
District Judge [   ] of the [   ] District Registry of the High Court

On [date of order]

21-02   Order of Request – Home Office

 **In the Principal Registry of the Family Division**

Case Number: FD09C00321

The full name(s) of the child(ren)	Boy or Girl	Date(s) of Birth
Samantha Draden	Girl	14.06.08

Order

Children Act 1989

UPON HEARING Counsel for the Applicant father

IT IS ORDERED THAT:-

1. In accordance with the President's Protocol of December 2002 the Home Office is requested to provide the following information (also detailed in the attached form EX660) to the court by 4pm on 26 November 2006:
    a. What is the current immigration status of Slavdic Curzanov?
    b. Does Slavdic Curzanov have any outstanding applications pending before the Home Office?

2. There be leave to disclose the case synopsis/summary/background to the Home Office.

3. There be permission granted for any information received from the Home Office to be disclosed to the parties.

Ordered by District Judge Red on the 29th day of October 2009

C21

21-03   Request Form – Home Office (Form EX660)

**Court request for information
to the Home Office
(Immigration and Nationality Directorate)**

Please note that all information provided in this
form will be forwarded to the Home Office

In the Principal Registry of the Family Division	
Case no.	
Serial no.	
Date	

In the matter of the   Act

In the matter of

To the judge: Each of the following fields must be completed to assist the Home Office to find the relevant records. Once completed pass the form to your Court Clerk. The Court Clerk will then produce a separate order directed to the Home Office, using the information provided on this form. The form must be sent **without delay** together with the court order to the Family Division Lawyer.

Name of Judge:					
Full name of each party, including relationship to child(ren)	Female/ Male (please tick)	Date of birth	Country of Origin	Date arrived In UK	All relevant Home Office Reference no's:
	☐ Female ☐ Male				
	☐ Female ☐ Male				
	☐ Female ☐ Male				
	☐ Female ☐ Male				
	☐ Female ☐ Male				
	☐ Female ☐ Male				

EX660 Court Request for information to the Home Office (02.06)   continued overleaf

Request Form - Home Office (Form EX660, page 2)

What questions would you like the IND to answer?	
Please provide a brief summary of case and any other information which will be useful to the IND in dealing with the request eg any details relating to immigration: (Please attach any documents, such as Case Summaries, in respect of which the Court has given leave to disclose to the Home Office).	

Has the court given leave to disclose any supporting documentation to the Home Office?	☐ **Yes**	☐ **No**
Contact details of person from whom additional information can be sought:		
By what date is the information required? (Please allow a minimum of 4 weeks. If the order cannot be sent to the President's Office on the day it is made please allow 6 weeks)		

To the court clerk
Please send this document, **together with the order** and any attached documents, **without delay** to:
Family Division Lawyer, President's Chambers, Royal Courts of Justice, Strand, London, WC2A 2LL
(tel: 020 7947 7197 fax: 020 7947 7274)

EX660 Court Request for information to the Home Office (02.06)   page 2

21-04   *Order of Request – General – Children*

In the Principal Registry of the Family Division

Case Number: FD09P02345

The full name(s) of the child(ren)	Boy or Girl	Date(s) of Birth
Brian Raleigh	Boy	25.11.07

Order

In the Matter of the Children Act 1989

UPON HEARING Counsel for the Applicant father

IT IS ORDERED THAT:-

1.   In accordance with the Registrar's Direction 1989 (as amended) the Department for Work and Pensions is requested to provide the following information to the court by 4 pm on 26 November 2009:

    (1)   what is the current or last known address of [*name(s) and date(s) of birth of person(s) sought*] (whose details are provided on the attached form)?

    (2)   *{ as appropriate }*

2.   The information is to be given in writing to an officer of the court, namely Ruth Ewen, Principal Registry of the Family Division, First Avenue House, 42-49 High Holborn, London WC1V 6NP.

3.   Any information received by the court under this order *{ delete as appropriate }*
[will be confidential to the court and may not be disclosed to the parties without permission of the court]
[may be disclosed to the parties].

4.   This order is made on condition that any information received will be used only for the purpose of service of the proceedings.

Ordered by District Judge Red of the Principal Registry of the Family Division

On the 29th day of October 2009

See Form 1 (Adapted EX660) attached to this Order

21-05   *Order of Request – General – Financial*

Case No: FD09D001234

IN THE HIGH COURT OF JUSTICE
In the Principal Registry of the Family Division

Matrimonial or civil partnership cause proceeding in the Principal Registry
treated by virtue of section 42 of the Matrimonial and Family Proceedings Act 1984
as pending in a divorce county court or civil partnership county court

BETWEEN	Brenda Mary CURTIS	Petitioner
AND	David Arnold CURTIS	Respondent

Before District Judge Blue sitting at the Principal Registry of the Family Division, First Avenue House, 42-49 High Holborn, London, WC1V 6NP 29th February 2009

UPON HEARING Counsel for the Petitioner

IT IS ORDERED THAT:-

1. In accordance with the Registrar's Direction 1989 (as amended) the Department for Work and Pensions is requested to provide the following information to the court by 4 pm on 29 March 2009:
    (1)   what is the current or last known address of [*name(s) and date(s) of birth of person(s) sought*] (whose details are provided on the attached form)?
    (2)   *{ as appropriate }*

2. The information is to be given in writing to an officer of the court, namely Ruth Ewen, Principal Registry of the Family Division, First Avenue House, 42-49 High Holborn, London WC1V 6NP.

3. Any information received by the court under this order *{delete as appropriate}*
    [will be confidential to the court and may not be disclosed to the parties without permission of the court]
    [may be disclosed to the parties].

4. This order is made because: *{delete as appropriate}*
    [a financial provision order is in existence, but cannot be enforced because the person against whom the order has been made cannot be traced]
    [the [petitioner] has filed or issued a notice, petition or originating summons containing an application for financial provision which cannot be served because the [respondent] cannot be traced].

5. This order is made on condition that any information received will be used only for the purpose of service of the proceedings.

See Form 1 (Adapted EX660) attached to this Order

21-06   *Request Form – General (Form 1: Adapted EX660)*

Court request for information

Please note that all information provided in this
form will be forwarded to the relevant department

In the Principal Registry of the Family Division	
Case no.	
Date	

In the matter of the   Act

In the matter of

To the judge: Please provide the following details (if known) of the person(s) about whom information is sought. Pass the completed form to the Court Clerk. The Court Clerk will then produce a separate order directed to the relevant department, using the information provided on this form

1	Surname
2	Forenames in full
3	National Insurance number
4	Female/Male (please tick) ☐ Female ☐ Male
5	Date of birth (or, if not known, approximate age)
6	Last known address, with date when living there
7	Any other known address(es) with dates
8	If the person sought is a war pensioner, his/her war pension and service particulars
9	The exact date of the marriage (or civil partnership)
10	Any previous names

Form 1 (Adapted from EX660) Court Request for information

21-07   *Request Form – General (Form 2)*

Case No: FD09D001234

IN THE HIGH COURT OF JUSTICE
In the Principal Registry of the Family Division

BETWEEN	Brenda Mary CURTIS	Petitioner
AND	David Arnold CURTIS	Respondent

COURT REQUEST FOR INFORMATION (ATTACHMENT TO ORDER)

Details (if known) of person sought:

1. National Insurance number

2. Surname

3. Forenames in full

4. Female/Male

5. Date of birth (or ,if not known, approximate age)

6. Last known address, with date when living there

7. Any other known address(es) with dates

8. If the person sought is a war pensioner, his/her war pension and service particulars

9. The exact date of the marriage or civil partnership and any previous names

_____

Dated

_____

Form 2 Court Request for information

21-08   Order – s 33 Family Law Act 1986

In the Principal Registry of the Family Division

Case Number: FD09P00321

Order

To disclose information about the whereabouts of a missing child
Section 33 Family Law Act 1986

The full name(s) of the child(ren)	Boy or Girl	Date(s) of Birth
Samantha Draden	Girl	14.06.08

The adult(s) who [is] [are] believed to have the child(ren) [is] [are]

Warning

Read this Order now. The Court has ordered you to give information and you must give it at once. If you do not, you may be in contempt of court and you may be fined, sent to prison or detained.

The Court orders
and directs

You

to give all the information you have about where the child(ren) and adult(s) are now, or where they were when you last knew
and where they are likely to be now.

You must give
the information

forthwith, that is as soon as practicable, to an officer of the court, namely Ruth Ewen, Principal Registry of the Family Division, First Avenue House, 42-49 High Holborn, London WC1V 6NP Principal Registry of the Family Division of the High Court

in the following way:
[   ]   in writing
[   ]   by attending before the court at *{address}*

on *{date}*   at *{time}*

Ordered by

District Judge Red of the Principal Registry of the Family Division

---

on

21-09   *Order of Request – General – Adoption (HM Forces)*

In the Principal Registry of the Family Division	
Case no. /Serial no.	**FD678/09**
Name of child	
Date	

In the Matter of the Adoption and Children Act 2002

Before District Judge Blue sitting at the Principal Registry of the Family Division, First Avenue House, 42-49 High Holborn, London, WC1V 6NP 29th February 2009

ON HEARING Counsel for the Applicants

IT IS ORDERED THAT:-

1.   Under the Family Procedure (Adoption) Rules 2005 Part 6 Practice Direction
    { insert name of person who is to answer the request }

    is requested to provide the following information to the court by 4 pm on 29 March 2009:
        what is the current or last known address of
        { name(s) and date(s) of birth of person(s) sought }

    (whose details are provided on the attached form)

2.   The information is to be given in writing to an officer of the court, namely Ruth Ewen, Principal Registry of the Family Division, First Avenue House, 42-49 High Holborn, London WC1V 6NP.

3.   Any information received by the court under this order *{delete as appropriate}*
    [will be confidential to the court and may not be disclosed to the parties without permission of the court]
    [may be disclosed to the parties].

4.   This order is made on condition that any information received will be used only for the purpose of issuing and service of the proceedings.

See Form HM Forces (Adapted EX660) attached to this Order

21-10 Request Form – Adoption (HM Forces: Adapted EX660)

Court request for information

In the Principal Registry of the Family Division	
Case no. / Serial no.	
Date	

Please note that all information provided in this form will be forwarded to the relevant department

In the matter of the Adoption and Children Act 2002

In the matter of

To the judge: Please provide the following details (if known) of the person(s) about whom information is sought. Pass the completed form to the Court Clerk. The Court Clerk will then produce a separate order directed to the relevant department, using the information provided on this form

1	Surname	
2	Forenames in full	
3	Service number	
4	Rank or rating	
5	Female/Male (please tick)	□ Female □ Male
6	Date of birth (or, if not known, approximate age)	
7	Ship, Arm or Trade, Regiment or Corps and Unit	
9	Last known address	
10	Other relevant information	

Form HM Forces (Adapted from EX660) Court Request for information

21-11   Order – Adoption and Children Act 2002 – Documents

In the Principal Registry of the Family Division	
Case no. /Serial no.	**FD678/09**
Name of child	
Date	

In the Matter of the Adoption and Children Act 2002

Before District Judge Blue sitting at the Principal Registry of the Family Division, First Avenue House, 42-49 High Holborn, London, WC1V 6NP 29th February 2009

ON HEARING Counsel for the Applicants

On the Application dated *{date}*
And on reading the evidence in   [the Application]
                             [the statement dated *{date}* made by *{name}*]

And under rule 79 of the Family Procedure (Adoption) Rules 2005

IT IS ORDERED THAT:-

1.   The respondent *{name}* must disclose a list of all of the following documents which are or were in his/her possession, custody or power:
   (1)   *{specify the documents or classes of documents}*
   (2)   . . . *{etc}*

2.   The respondent *{name}* must specify a list of any of the documents identified in paragraph 1 of this order:
   (1)   which are no longer in his/her/its control; or
   (2)   in respect of which he/she/it claims a right or duty to withhold inspection

3.   The respondent must by *{time and date}* send the list of documents to the [legal advisers of] the Applicant [at *{address}*.

4.   The respondent must by *{time and date}* produce [copies of] the documents to [the Applicant] [the legal advisers of the Applicant] [the medical or professional adviser of the Applicant] namely *{name and address}*.

5.   The order to produce the documents is made subject to the following condition(s):
   (1)   [the medical records are not to be disclosed to the Applicant] *{or as appropriate}*
   (2)   . . . *{etc}*

6.   The respondent may apply to set aside or vary this order within 7 days of the date on which this order was served on him/her/it.

21-12 *Order Menu – Directions (Financial Ancillary Relief)*

Case Name   Case Number   FD   D

[Deputy] District Judge   Date

Attendance etc	N/A	I/P	Csl	Solr	(Other - specify)
Petitioner	☐	☐	☐	☐	☐
Respondent	☐	☐	☐	☐	☐

Notice of Hearing   ☐   Without notice   ☐   On notice

Hearing   ☐   First Appointment   ☐   FDR Appointment

Application[s] dated

.

Maintenance Pending Suit/Outcome Hearing

[ ]   The application for maintenance pending suit/outcome is listed for hearing before

    ☐   DJ PRFD   ☐   CJ PRFD   ☐   HCJ RCJ

    on   at   (time estimate   )

    and the following directions shall apply

    [ ]   The application will be heard without oral evidence [unless the Court directs

        otherwise].

    [ ]   The [Petitioner] [and the] [Respondent] may [must] [each] file and serve

        by 4.00pm on   a concise sworn statement.

    [ ]   The [Petitioner] [and the] [Respondent] may [must] [each] file and serve

        by 4.00pm on   a concise sworn statement in answer.

    [ ]   The [Petitioner] [Respondent] may file and serve

        by 4.00pm on   a concise sworn statement in reply.

    [ ]   The sworn statements shall be limited to the issues relevant to maintenance

        pending suit/outcome.

    [ ]   A trial bundle and other documents in accordance with the rules and current

        practice direction must be lodged with the court by 4.00pm on

Order Menu - Directions (Financial Ancillary Relief) (page 2)

| Forms E and other Documents |

[   ]   The [Petitioner] *{name}*   [and] [Respondent] *{name}*

must [each] file and serve a completed and sworn Form E

[by 4.00pm on   ]

[and if not done by that date then] [within   [days] of service of this

order on [him] [her]]

[   ]   The [Petitioner] *{name}*   [and] [Respondent] *{name}*

must [each] file and serve a [statement of issues] [chronology] [and] [any

questionnaire] [by 4.00pm on   ]

| Questionnaires |

[   ]   The Petitioner and Respondent must each provide to the other by 4.00 pm on

                                    the information and copy documents requested in the

respective questionnaires [as amended by the court] [except for reasonable objections]

[   ]   The Petitioner must provide to the Respondent [by 4.00 pm on   ]

[and if not done by that date then] [within   days of service of this order on

[him] [her]] the information and copy documents requested in the Respondent's

questionnaire dated

☐   [as amended by the court]

☐   [limited as follows] [except for reasonable objections]

[   ]   The Respondent must provide to the Petitioner [by 4.00 pm on   ]

[and if not done by that date then] [within   days of service of this order on

[him] [her]] the information and copy documents requested in the Petitioner's

questionnaire dated

☐   [as amended by the court]

☐   [limited as follows] [except for reasonable objections]

Order Menu - Directions (Financial Ancillary Relief) (page 3)

[   ]   The parties must not file with the court the replies to questionnaires unless the court specifically so directs.

Valuation of property

[   ]   The value[s] of the [property] [properties] known as

be agreed if possible, but where any value is not agreed the following directions shall apply

    [   ]   [The] [Each] property be valued by a written report [in the form of a market appraisal] from a single joint valuer [for each property] agreed between the parties [or, if not agreed, selected by the court]

    [   ]   The report[s] [is] [are] to be disclosed to each party by 4.00pm on

    [   ]   [If no single joint valuer is agreed] Each party may use the evidence of one valuer [for each property] whose report, if relied on, is to be disclosed to the other party

        [by 4.00pm on   ]

        [no later than   weeks before the final hearing]

    [   ]   If there is more than one valuer for a property, those valuers are to consult together

        [by 4.00pm on   ]

        [no later than   weeks before the final hearing]

        to identify any points of agreement and disagreement.

    [   ]   The report[s] [is] [are] to be received in evidence without the attendance of the valuer[s].

Order Menu - Directions (Financial Ancillary Relief) (page 4)

Experts : Accountants etc

[   ]   The [Petitioner] [and] [Respondent] may [each] use the expert evidence of [one]

[jointly appointed] [accountant]

on the question[s] of

and the following directions shall apply

[   ]   The solicitor for the [Petitioner] [Respondent]

is to be the lead solicitor for the purpose of the instruction of the joint expert.

[   ]   The [Petitioner] [Respondent]

is to provide a draft letter of instruction to the [Petitioner] [Respondent]

by 4.00pm on

and any comments on the draft letter are to be provided to the [Petitioner]

[Respondent] by 4.00pm on

[   ]   Any report relied on [by the [Petitioner] [Respondent]] must be disclosed to

[each party] [the other party] [the] [Respondent] [Petitioner]

by 4.00 pm on

[   ]   Any report relied on [by the [Respondent] [Petitioner]] must be disclosed to [each

party] [the other party] [the] [Petitioner] [Respondent] by 4.00 pm on

[   ]   The experts are to consult together

[by 4.00pm on   ]

[no later than   weeks before the final hearing]

to identify any points of agreement and disagreement.

[   ]   The report[s] [is] [are] to be received in evidence without the attendance of the

expert[s].

Order Menu - Directions (Financial Ancillary Relief) (page 5)

| Transfer / Interim Hearings |

[ ]   The [suit] [application[s] [is] [are] transferred to the High Court.

[ ]   The application[s] for   [is] [are] listed for a [mention]

[further] [first appointment] [financial dispute resolution appointment] [directions]

[hearing] before

    ☐   DJ PRFD   ☐ CJ PRFD   ☐   HCJ RCJ

on   at   (time estimate   )

[ ]   The mention date may be vacated if before then a consent minute has been lodged

and approved by the court

[ ]   Both parties and their legal advisers (if any) must attend court on

at   for the purpose of negotiation.

[ ]   The personal attendance of [both] the [Petitioner] [Respondent] [is] [are] excused

provided that [his] [her] [their] legal representative[s] attend[s] with full instructions.

[ ]   There shall be no financial dispute resolution appointment.

| Directions for Final Hearing |

[ ]   The application[s] for   [is] [are] listed for [final] hearing

before

    ☐   DJ PRFD   ☐ CJ PRFD   ☐   HCJ RCJ

on   at   (time estimate   )

☐ with judicial reading time of   [hours] [day] from the start of the hearing

[ ]   Each party [must] [may] file and serve by 4.00pm on

a concise narrative sworn statement limited to

[the relevant matters in issue between the parties]

[the issue[s] of]

[ ]   No further statements may be filed without the permission of the court.

[ ]   Both parties are to attend the final hearing for cross examination.

Order Menu - Directions (Financial Ancillary Relief) (page 6)

[ ]   A trial bundle and other documents in accordance with the rules and current practice

direction must be lodged with the court by 4.00pm on

| Other Orders |

□   Continued on Another Sheet

[ ]   **| Costs |**

      □   No order as to costs   □   Costs in the application   □   Costs reserved

      □   Funded Services Assessment of the costs of the

      □   (Other - specify)

| NOTE (not part of the order) |

□   Penal notice addressed to [Respondent]   attached to paragraph(s)

Dated: (Signed)   DJ

21-13   *Order Menu – Non Molestation Order (Family Law Act 1996)*

(NO POWER OF ARREST)

Case Name   Case Number   FD   F

[Deputy] District Judge   Date

Attendance etc	N/A	I/P	Csl	Solr	(Other - specify)
Applicant	☐	☐	☐	☐	☐
Respondent	☐	☐	☐	☐	☐

Notice of Hearing   ☐   Without notice   ☐   On notice

Application[s] dated

Evidence read   *{Statement/Affidavit/Report   Maker/Author   Date}*

| Definitions |

[   ]   In this order the Applicant is *{name}*

[   ]   In this order the Respondent is *{name}*

[   ]   In this order the child[ren] [is] [are] *{name(s)}*

| **Non Molestation (Applicant) – s 42 FLA 1996 - No Power of Arrest** |

[   ]   The Respondent is forbidden to

    [   ]   use or threaten violence against the Applicant and must not instruct or

        encourage any other person to do so;

    [   ]   intimidate or harass the Applicant and must not instruct or encourage any other

        person to do so;

    [   ]   telephone, text , email or otherwise contact or attempt to contact the Applicant

        except for the purpose of making arrangements for contact between the

        Respondent and the child[ren]

Order Menu - Non Molestation Order (page 2)

[   ]   telephone, text , email or otherwise contact or attempt to contact the Applicant

[except through his/her solicitors *{name, address & telephone number}*]

[   ]   damage, attempt to damage or threaten to damage any property owned by or in

the possession or control of the Applicant and must not instruct or encourage

any other person to do so;

[   ]   damage, attempt to damage or threaten to damage any property jointly owned by

the Applicant and Respondent or in their joint possession or control and must not

instruct or encourage any other person to do so;

[   ]   damage, attempt to damage or threaten to damage the property or contents of

the property known as *{address}*

and must not instruct or encourage any other person to do so

[   ]   *{Other – see attached sheet}*

Zonal Non Molestation – No Power of Arrest

[   ]   The Respondent must not go to, enter or attempt to enter

    [   ]   any property where he knows or believes the Applicant to be living

    [   ]   the property known as *{address}*

    [   ]   or go within   [metres] of it

    [   ]   or go onto or along the road(s) known as

    [   ]   except that the Respondent may go to the property [without entering it] for the

purpose only of such contact with any child[ren] as may be agreed in writing

between the Applicant and Respondent or ordered by the court.

Order Menu - Non Molestation Order (page 3)

| Rights of Occupation – Suspension |

{If the Respondent has rights of occupation, but is not in actual occupation, then this paragraph may be completed to run for the same period as the exclusion order, but without any power of arrest. It is declaratory not injunctive}

[ ]   The Court declares that the right of the Respondent *{name}* to remain in occupation of the property known as *{address}*

shall be suspended

    [ ]   during the period of the exclusion order under paragraph [ ] of this order

    [ ]   until *{or time and date}*

| Non Molestation (Children) – No Power of Arrest |

[ ]   The Respondent is forbidden to

    [ ]   use or threaten violence against the child[ren] and must not instruct or encourage any other person to do so;

    [ ]   intimidate or harass the child[ren] and must not instruct or encourage any other person to do so;

    [ ]   telephone, text, email or otherwise contact or attempt to contact the child[ren] except for such contact as may be agreed in writing between the Applicant and Respondent or ordered by the court.

[ ]   The Respondent must not [between the hours of 8.30am and 4.00pm] go to, enter or attempt to enter the school premises known as *{address}*

    [ ]   or go within   [metres] of it

    [ ]   or go onto or along the road(s) known as

    [ ]   except by prior written invitation from the school authorities

Order Menu - Non Molestation Order (page 4)

Duration of Non Molestation Order

[   ]   Paragraph(s)   of this order shall begin from the time that

    [   ]   it is personally served on the Respondent

    [   ]   the Respondent is made aware of the terms of this order whether by personal

          service or otherwise.

[   ]   [Paragraph[s]   of this] [This] order shall last until

[further order] *{or time and date}*

[unless before then it is varied or revoked by an order of the court].

[   ]   The Respondent may apply to vary or revoke this order on   [hours] [days]

written notice.

Transfer / Hearings

[   ]   The application[s] [is] [are] transferred to the [Inner London]   FPC.

[   ]   The application(s) for injunction orders [is] [are] listed for [further] [directions] [hearing]

before

    ☐ DJ PRFD   ☐ CJ PRFD   ☐ Inner London FPC

on   at   (time estimate   )

Other Orders

❑   **Continued on Another Sheet**

[   ]   **Costs**

    ☐   Costs reserved   ☐   Costs in the application

    ☐   No order as to costs

    ☐   Funded Services Assessment of the costs of the [Applicant] [and] [Respondent]

    ☐   (Other - specify)

Dated: (Signed)   DJ

21-14   Order Menu – Occupation Order (Family Law Act 1996)

(POWER OF ARREST MAY BE ATTACHED)

Case Name   Case Number   FD   F

[Deputy] District Judge   Date

Attendance etc	N/A	I/P	Csl	Solr	(Other - specify)
Applicant	☐	☐	☐	☐	☐
Respondent	☐	☐	☐	☐	☐

Notice of Hearing   ☐   Without notice   ☐   On notice

Application[s] dated

Evidence read   *{Statement/Affidavit/Report*   *Maker/Author*   *Date}*

| Occupation Rights - if there is No Existing Right to Occupy |

{Length of order – Not more than 6 months, plus (one extension of 6 months, if

cohabitant) or (more than one extension, if former spouse)}

[ ]   *{Applicant in occupation}* The Applicant *{name}* has the right not to be evicted or excluded

from the property known as *{address}*

or any part of it by the Respondent *{name}* until *{time and date}*

and the Respondent shall not evict or exclude the Applicant during that period.

[ ]   *{Applicant not in occupation}* The Applicant *{name}* has the right to enter into and occupy

the property known as *{address}*

until *{time and date}*

and the Respondent *{name}* shall allow the Applicant to do so.

Order Menu - Occupation Order (page 2)

Home Rights - Continuation

[   ]   The Court declares that the home rights of the Applicant *{name}* in the property known

as *{address}*

shall not end when the Respondent *{name}* dies or their marriage/civil partnership is

dissolved and shall continue until

[the determination of the financial ancillary relief claims in Petition Number   ]

{or time and date}   [or] [further order]

Rights of Occupation – Suspension

[   ]   The Court declares that the right of the Respondent *{name}* to remain in occupation of the

property known as *{address}*

shall be suspended until

[the determination of the financial ancillary relief claims in Petition Number   ]

{or time and date}   [or] [further order]

Occupation Order – Power of Arrest May be Attached

[   ]   The Respondent *{name}* shall allow the Applicant *{name}* sole occupation [of part] of

the property known as *{address}*

[namely] *{identify part}*

[and the Respondent shall not enter or attempt to enter [that part] [of] [that property]

[and the Respondent shall allow the Applicant shared use of the common parts of the

property]

Order Menu - Occupation Order (page 3)

[　]　The Respondent *{name}* shall leave the property known as *{address}*

    [　]　by *{time}*   on *{day and date}*

    [　]　[immediately on]　[within   [days] [hours] of]

       service of this order on [him] [her].

[　]　Having left the property known as *{address}*

the Respondent *{name}* must not return to, enter or attempt to enter it

    [　]　or go within   [metres] of it

    [　]　or go onto or along the road(s) known as

    [　]　except that the Respondent may go to the property [without entering it] for the

purpose only of such contact with any relevant child[ren] as may be agreed [in writing]

between the parties or ordered by the court.

Duration of Occupation Order

[　]　Paragraph(s)   of this order shall begin from the time that

    [　]　it is personally served on the Respondent

    [　]　the Respondent is made aware of the terms of this order whether by personal

       service or otherwise.

[　]　[Paragraph[s]   of this] [This] order shall last until

[further order] *{or time and date}*

[unless before then it is varied or revoked by an order of the court].

[　]　The Respondent may apply to vary or revoke this order on   [hours] [days]

written notice.

Order Menu - Occupation Order (page 4)

| Power of Arrest – Attached only to Occupation Orders |

[   ]   A power of arrest is attached to paragraph[s]   of this order.

[   ]   The power of arrest shall last until *{time and date}*

| Transfer / Hearings |

[   ]   The application[s] [is] [are] transferred to the [Inner London]   FPC.

[   ]   The application(s) for injunction orders [is] [are] listed for [further] [directions] [hearing]

before

☐ DJ PRFD   ☐ CJ PRFD   ☐ Inner London FPC

on   at   (time estimate   )

| Other Orders |

❑   **Continued on Another Sheet**

[   ] | Costs |

☐   Costs reserved   ☐   Costs in the application

☐   No order as to costs

☐   Funded Services Assessment of the costs of the [Applicant] [and] [Respondent]

☐   (Other - specify)

Dated: (Signed)   DJ

21-15   *Order Menu – Prohibited Steps, Directions (s 8 Children Act 1989)*

Case Name: Case Number: FD   P

[Deputy] District Judge   Date

Attendance etc	N/A	I/P	Csl	Solr	(Other - specify)
Applicant	☐	☐	☐	☐	☐
Respondent	☐	☐	☐	☐	☐

Notice of Hearing   ☐   Without notice   ☐   On notice

Hearing   ☐   Conciliation   ☐   Directions

Application[s] dated

Evidence read   *{Statement/Affidavit/Report*   *Maker/Author*   *Date}*

Prohibited Steps

[ ]   The Respondent [F] [M] *{name}*
        must not remove [any of] the child[ren] *{name(s)}*

    [ ]   from England and Wales

    [ ]   from the care of the Applicant *{name}*

       [or from [his] [her] [their] address known as]

    [ ]   from [his] [her] [their] [respective] school[s] known as

    [ ]   *{other}*

    [ ]   [except for such contact as the parties may agree in writing or as may be ordered
       by the court]

[without the [written consent of the Applicant or] the consent of the court]

[and must not instruct or encourage any other person to do so].

Order Menu - Prohibited Steps and Directions (page 2)

| Duration of Order |

[   ]   [Paragraph[s]   of this] [This] order shall last until [further order]

    {or time and date}

    [unless before then it is varied or discharged by an order of the court].

[   ]   The Respondent may apply to vary or discharge this order on   [hours] [days]

    written notice.

| Penal Notice |

[   ]   A penal notice addressed to [the Respondent] *{name}*

    be attached to paragraph[s]   of this order

| CAFCASS and Local Authority Section 7 Reports |

[   ]   A children and family reporter [*{name}*   if available]

    is directed to report on the question[s] of [residence] [and] [contact]

    {or as appropriate}

    and to file the report by 4.00pm on

    and at the same time provide each of the parties or their solicitors with a copy of the

    report.

[   ]   Under s 7(1)(b) CA 1989, *{LA name}*

    is requested to appoint a welfare officer [*{name}*   if available]

    to report on the question[s] of [residence] [and] [contact]

    [the circumstances of the child[ren]]

    and to file the report by 4.00pm on

    and at the same time provide each of the parties or their solicitors with a copy of the

    report.

| Local Authority Investigation under s 37 Children Act 1989 |

☐   *{Complete s 37 Order Menu Form}*

Order Menu - Prohibited Steps and Directions (page 3)

Disclosure of Documents

[   ]   The following documents are to be disclosed to the [children and family reporter] [Social

Services Department of the Local Authority] for the purpose of the report:

[   ]   [all orders, applications, statements and reports filed]

[   ]   *{Application/Statement/Report*   *Applicant/Maker/Author*   *{Date}*

Attendance of Reporter at Hearings

[   ]   The reporting officer is requested to attend the [directions] hearing before

☐ DJ PRFD   ☐ CJ PRFD   ☐ HCJ RCJ

on   at

[for the purpose of giving a[n] [short] oral report]

[   ]   The reporting officer is requested to note the date of the final hearing and be available to

attend if requested to do so by either party in writing by 4.00pm on

Experts

[   ]   The [M] [and] [F]   may [jointly] instruct

a [psychologist] [consultant [child and adolescent] psychiatrist]

for the purpose of a report on

such report to be filed and served by 4.00pm on

☐ with   ☐ without   leave to examine and assess the child[ren].

[   ]   The [M] [F]   [is] [are] to provide a draft letter of instruction to

[all] [the] other [party] [parties]   by 4.00pm on

and any comments on the draft letter are to be provided

to the instructing [party] [parties] by 4.00pm on

Order Menu - Prohibited Steps and Directions (page 4)

Evidence

[   ]   The [M]   [F]   [is] [are] [may] [each] [to] file and serve

by 4.00pm on

[a] [the] [statement[s]   [all] [evidence]   on which [it] [he] [she] [each]

intends to rely

[including]

[   ]   The [M]   [F]   [is] [are] [may] [each] [to] file and serve

by 4.00pm on

[a] [the] [statement[s]   [all] [evidence]   on which [it] [he] [she] [each]

intends to rely

[including]

[   ]   The [M]   [F]   [is] [are] [may] [each] [to] file and serve by 4.00pm on

any [statement[s] [evidence] [in answer].

[   ]   The [statements] [evidence] shall be limited to the issue[s] of

Transfer / Hearings

[   ]   The application[s] [is] [are] transferred to the

☐ High Court   ☐ Inner London FPC.

[   ]   The application[s] for   [is] [are] listed for

[further] [directions] [hearing]   before

☐ DJ PRFD   ☐ CJ PRFD   ☐ HCJ RCJ   ☐ Inner London FPC

on   at   (time estimate   )

[   ]   A trial bundle and other documents in accordance with the current practice direction must

be lodged with the court by 4.00pm on

Menu Form - Prohibited Steps and Directions (page 5)

❑   **Continued on Another Sheet**

[ ]   Costs

  ☐   No order as to costs   ☐   Costs in the application   ☐   Costs reserved

  ☐   Funded Services Assessment of the costs of the

  ☐   (Other - specify)

Dated: (Signed)   DJ

21-16   *Order Menu – Local Authority Investigation (s 37 Children Act 1989)*

Case Name: Case Number: FD   P

[Deputy] HHJ/DJ   Date

❑   **Attached to Main Order Menu**

| **Local Authority Investigation under section 37 Children Act 1989** |

[   ]   Under section 37 CA 1989, it appearing to the Court that it may be appropriate for a care

or supervision order to be made in respect of the child[ren]

{Identify the child(ren) to whom the direction applies}

a [boy] [girl] born on

a [boy] [girl] born on

a [boy] [girl] born on

the Court directs the *{LA name}*

to investigate the circumstances of the child[ren].

| **Filing and Serving the Report** |

[   ]   Under section 37 CA 1989, the local authority must report to the Court, in writing, by

4.00pm on

[and at the same time provide each of the parties or their solicitors with a copy of the

report.]

| **Attendance of Reporter at Hearings** |

[   ]   A representative of the local authority is requested to attend the [directions] hearing

before

❑ DJ PRFD   ❑ CJ PRFD   ❑ HCJ RCJ

on   at   (time estimate   )

[for the purpose of giving a[n] [short] oral report]

Order Menu - Local Authority Investigation (s 37 Children Act 1989) (page 2)

| Disclosure of Documents |

[   ]   The Court directs copies of the following documents shall be served on the local authority

(namely):

    [   ]   [all orders, applications, statements and reports filed]

    [   ]   *{Application/Statement/Report*   *Applicant/Maker/Author*   *Date}*

| Appointment of Children's Guardian (only with s.37 direction) |

[   ]   The Court [having made] [considering whether to make] an interim care order, a

children's guardian shall be appointed for the child[ren]

| Interim Care Order |

[   ]   The child[ren] *{give their names etc}*

                                  a [boy] [girl] born on

                                  a [boy] [girl] born on

                                  a [boy] [girl] born on

be placed in the interim care of *{name of Local Authority}*

The interim care order expires on *{time and date}*

Dated: (Signed)   HHJ/DJ

21-17   *Order Menu – Case Management Directions (Public Law Outline)*

Case Name: Case No. FD   C
                                                             Child(ren) No.

The High Court sitting at [   ]

The Principal Registry of the Family Division

[   ] Family Proceedings / County Court

Mr/Mrs Justice/HHJ/District Judge   Date

Attendance etc	N/A	I/P	Csl	Solr	(Other - specify)
Applicant [LA]	☐	☐	☐	☐	☐
Respondent (1) [M]	☐	☐	☐	☐	☐
Respondent (2) [F]	☐	☐	☐	☐	☐
Respondent (3)	☐	☐	☐	☐	☐
Respondent (4)	☐	☐	☐	☐	☐
Respondent [Children's Guardian (CG)]	☐	☐	☐	☐	☐

Appointment of the Official Solicitor

[   ]   The Official Solicitor is appointed (if he consents) to act in these proceedings on behalf of

the [M] [F] *{name}*   .

Joining Respondents to Meet Allegations

[   ]   (1)   The person(s) named in this paragraph [is] [are] joined as [a] Respondent[s] to

these proceedings in order to meet the allegation(s) that the

[injuries to] [sexual abuse of] *{other}*

the child[ren] *{name(s)}*

may have been caused by [him] [her] [them or one of them] or that [he] [she] [they or

one of them] may have failed to protect the child[ren]

[   ]   (2)   The person(s) named and joined [is] [are]

as [4th] [5th] [6th]   Respondent

as [4th] [5th] [6th]   Respondent

Order Menu - Case Management Directions (PLO) (page 2)

[   ]   (3)   [Disclosure of documents to the person(s) named in this paragraph shall]

[be limited to] [the following] [those necessary to]

[exclude]

| Statements |

[   ]   The [LA]   shall file and serve

    [   ]   by 4.00pm on *{date}*

        [   ]   a social work assessment of

        [   ]   a[n] [updated] chronology

        [   ]   its [outline] [interim] [final] care plan(s)]

        [   ]

    [   ]   by 4.00pm on *{date}*

        [   ]   a statement [not exceeding [4]   A4 pages] [on the question of]

        [   ]   *{other}*

        [   ]

        [   ]

    [   ]   by 4.00pm on *{date}*

        [   ]   all other evidence on which it intends to rely [including its final care plan(s)]

[   ]   The [M] [F] [CG]   [shall] [may] [each] file and serve

    [   ]   by 4.00pm on *{date}*

        [   ]   a statement [not exceeding [4] A4 pages] [on the question of]

        [   ]   *{other}*

        [   ]

        [   ]

    [   ]   by 4.00pm on *{date}*

        [   ]   [all other evidence on which [it] [he] [she] [each] intends to rely]

Menu Form - Case Management Directions (PLO) (page 3)

[   ]   The Children's Guardian shall file and serve

by 4.00pm on *{date}*

    [   ]   a[n] [outline] [interim] report [not exceeding [4]   A4 pages]

    [   ]   [his] [her] [final] [analysis] [report]

    [   ]   *{other}*

Threshold Criteria Schedules

[   ]   The [LA]   shall file and serve by 4.00pm on

a concise schedule of the findings it seeks on the threshold criteria

[   ]   The [M] [F] [CG]   shall [each] file and serve by 4.00pm on

concise particulars of the answer and any admissions of that party on the threshold

criteria

Identifying Kinship or Alternative Carers

[   ]   If the [M] or [F]   proposes that kinship or alternative carers for the

child(ren) should be considered or assessed, the names and addresses of those

proposed carers must be provided to the local authority by *{date}*

Disclosure of Police Records

[   ]   If the [LA] [M] [F] [any party]   intends to obtain or rely on records or statements

held by the police [it/he/she/that party]   shall by 4.00pm on *{date}*

make a written request to the police for disclosure under the relevant police protocol, and

(if obtained) shall not file them with the court but shall within [7]   days of disclosure

serve copies of such documents on the other parties.

Disclosure of Medical Records

[   ]   If the [LA] [M] [F] [any party]   intends to obtain or rely on medical records or

notes held by *{name of hospital or GP/doctor}*

[it/he/she/that party]   shall by 4.00pm on *{date}*

make a written request to the [hospital] [doctor] for disclosure and (if obtained) shall not

file them with the court but shall within [7]   days of disclosure serve copies of

such documents on :-

Menu Form - Case Management Directions (PLO) (page 4)

[   ] [the other parties]

[   ] [in the first instance, only the expert(s) *{name(s)}*

[   ] [it being recorded that the [M] [F] *{other} {name}*

consents to such disclosure]

| Experts |

[   ] (See separate sheet)

| Advocates Meeting |

[   ] The parties' lawyers and any unrepresented party shall

    [   ] attend an Advocates Meeting at *{place}*

        on *{date}*   at *{time}*   [am][pm]

        to prepare a draft case management order   [and]

    [   ] attend court on *{date}*   at *{time}*   [am] [pm]

        for the purpose of complying with the Public Law Outline.

| Hearings |

[   ] The application[s] [for] [interim] [care] [or] [supervision] order(s) [is] [are] listed for

a [further] [directions]   [hearing]   before

☐ Inner London FPC   ☐ DJ PRFD   ☐ CJ [PRFD] [Gee St]   ☐ HCJ RCJ

on   at   (time estimate   )

☐ with judicial reading time of   [hours] [day] from the start of the hearing

☐ (at risk)   ☐ [allocated judge] [reserved to]   [if available].

[   ] The application[s] [for] [a] [care] [or] [supervision] order(s) [is] [are] listed for

[a fact finding hearing] [on the question(s) of]

before

☐ Inner London FPC   ☐ DJ PRFD   ☐ CJ [PRFD [Gee St]   ☐ HCJ RCJ

on   at   (time estimate   )

☐ with judicial reading time of   [hours] [day] from the start of the hearing

☐ (at risk)   ☐ [allocated judge] [reserved to]   [if available].

Menu Form - Case Management Directions (PLO) (page 5)

[ ] The application[s] [for] [a] [care] [or] [supervision] order(s) [is] [are] listed for

an [Issues Resolution Hearing]   before

☐ Inner London FPC   ☐ DJ PRFD   ☐ CJ [PRFD] [Gee St]   ☐ HCJ RCJ

on   at   (time estimate [2]   [hours] day(s)])

☐ with judicial reading time of   [hours] [day] from the start of the hearing

☐ (at risk)   ☐ [allocated judge] [reserved to]   [if available].

[ ] The application[s] [for] [a] [care] [or] [supervision] order(s) [is] [are] listed for

[final hearing]

before

☐ Inner London FPC   ☐ DJ PRFD   ☐ CJ [PRFD [Gee St]   ☐ HCJ RCJ

on   at   (time estimate   )

☐ with judicial reading time of   [hours] [day] from the start of the hearing

☐ (at risk)   ☐ [allocated judge] [reserved to]   [if available].

Controlling Unnecessary Filing of General Documentary Disclosure

[ ] General documentary disclosure (including health records, education records, police

records, contact notes and Local Authority minutes) must not be filed with the court,

unless the court specifically so directs.

Other Directions

Dated: (Signed)   HHJ/DJ

21-18   *Order Menu – Instruction of Experts (Public Law Outline)*

Case Name: Case No. FD   C
                                                             Child(ren) No.

The High Court sitting at [   ]

The Principal Registry of the Family Division

[   ] Family Proceedings / County Court

Mr/Mrs Justice/HHJ/DJ   Date

☐   **Attach to main Order Menu Form**

| Experts |

[   ]   The [LA] [M] [F] [CG]   may [jointly] instruct

a [psychologist] [consultant] [adult] [child and adolescent] [psychiatrist]

[relevant staff at   ]

for the purpose of a[n] [viability] [residential] [assessment and] report on

such report to be filed and served by 4.00pm on

☐ with   ☐ without   leave to examine and assess the child[ren].

[   ]   The solicitor for [LA] [M] [F] [CG]

is to be the lead solicitor for the purpose of the instruction of the expert.

[   ]   The [LA] [M] [F] [CG]   [is] [are] to provide a draft letter of instruction to all other

parties by 4.00pm on

and any comments on the draft letter are to be provided to the [other parties]

by 4.00pm on

[   ]   The letter of instruction is to be sent to the expert(s) by 4.00pm on *{date}*

[   ]   The reasonable cost of the report [and] [viability] [assessment] shall be

[apportioned equally between the [instructing] parties and such costs shall be] a proper

charge on the public funding certificate(s) of [those parties who have such a certificate]

[M] [F] [CG]

Order Menu - Instruction of Expert (Public Law Outline) (page 2)

| Consultation by Experts |

[   ]   The experts are to consult together

[by 4.00pm on   ]

[no later than   weeks before the final hearing]

to identify any points of agreement and disagreement, and are to provide the parties with

a note of such points by   .

| Enquiries about Assessments |

[   ]   The [LA] [M] [F] [CG]

may [each] disclose documents on a confidential basis to

[   ] [relevant staff at   ]

[   ] [not more than [2] [   ] [psychiatrists] [psychologists] [independent social workers]

[   ] {other}

for the purpose of enquiries to identify the suitability and availability of

[   ] a[n] [residential] [parenting] assessment of the [parents] [M] [F] [and child(ren)]

[   ] a risk assessment of

[   ] {other}

Dated: (Signed)   HHJ/DJ